P9-BZS-685

THE PEACH SAMPLER

compiled by Eliza Mears Horton
First Edition

Edited by Anna Hicks
Cover designed and stitched by Parke B. Horton
Section pages designed and stitched by Tracy M. Horton

Copyright © 1983 by Eliza Mears Horton

All rights reserved.

International Standard Book Number – 0-9609966-0-5

Library of Congress Catalog Card Number: 82-90973

Published by: At Home Enterprises

This book is bound with the finest plastic binders available, but like most plastics, can be damaged by excessive heat. Care should be taken to avoid exposing them to the direct rays of the sun for extended periods of time, or excessive heat such as in a car on a hot day, or on the top of the kitchen stove. If not over exposed to heat, the binders will last indefinitely.

All recipes carefully edited by Lib Bouknight and Betty Rountree, Home Economists

Peach design on cover used by permission of The Steele Family, Sumter, S.C.

First Printing 1983
Second Printing 1984
Third Printing 1987
Fourth Printing 1990
Fifth Printing 1994

Printed in the USA by

WIMMER
The Wimmer Companies, Inc.
Memphis • Dallas

For additional copies of
"The Peach Sampler"
Please send $9.95
plus $2.00 postage and handling
per book to:
THE PEACH SAMPLER
829 Mallard Lakes Drive
Lexington, SC 29072
Telephone 803-356-6208

to the wonderful memory of my mother who taught me to love God, family, country and peaches....
and
to Willard Charlton Horton, Jr.
my husband, who wouldn't let me quit until "the book" was finished!

The Author wishes to thank and give credit to:

The California Tree Fruit Agreement
The Georgia Peach Commission
The National Peach Council
The South Carolina Department of Agriculture and
The South Carolina Peach Council who gave permission to use their recipes. The recipes are printed as submitted and individual credit is given with each recipe and in the index. The National Peach Council granted permission to use its photographs.
The South Carolina Peach Council for its endorsement and support.

Evelyn Beauly . . . . "The Apple Book"
Salisbury, New Hampshire

Lib Bouknight . . . . Home Economist
Irmo, SC

Priscilla Bundrick . . . . Commercial Art Instructor
Lexington Vocational Center

Peggie L. Davis . . . . Home Economist
SC Department of Agriculture

Vonnie Doughty . . . . Graphic Consultant
Gilbert, SC

Larry Drake . . . . Graphic Instructor
Lexington Vocational Center

Mark Ethridge . . . . Professor, School of Journalism
University of South Carolina

Gene Hall . . . . Marketing Specialist
SC Department of Agriculture

Anna Hicks . . . . English Teacher
Irmo High School

Lillie Hoover . . . . Executive Director,
National Peach Council,
Martinsburg, W VA

Betty Rountree . . . . Home Economist
Lexington, SC

Rick Taylor . . . . Art Consultant, Omni Studios
West Columbia, SC

Larry Yonce . . . . President
SC Peach Council and Promotion Board
Johnston, SC

Bonnie Carroll, Jean Carter, Mary Getts, Estelle Morgan, Marolyn Proctor, Bobbi Sox and DeeDee Whitehead—proof readers.

and those too numerous to name who gave valuable assistance, support and encouragement.

Table of Contents

My Recipe

I have a recipe for life,
The best one that I know;
I guarantee the end result...
'Twas taught me long ago!

You start by mixing just a dash
Of humor with the day,
And then you add a cheery smile
As you go on your way.

Love's never out of season
So you add a large amount,
And I never measure sympathy;
You don't with things that count.

Toss in a bit of effort
And a lot of nerve and grit,
And hope makes all the difference,
For a thing improves with it.

You stir a bit of kindness in,
Along with patience, too,
And flavor it with gentleness
Whatever you may do.

And when the sun is setting,
You'll look back in joy to see
A worthwhile product of your toil
...Within my recipe!

Grace E. Easley

Hail to the Peach

A peach is a peach is a peach—not so as peach lovers will attest. Webster defines a peach as "a small tree with lance-shaped leaves, pink flowers, and round, juicy, orange-yellow fruit, with a fuzzy skin and a single, rough pit," but to really understand what a peach is, one must experience the sight, the fragrance, the touch and especially the taste! A good graphic description of a peach might be a "stone fruit"

virtually without stems, oval in outline, averaging 2 to 3 inches in diameter. Colors range from occasional pure white through shades of pink to deep red. The flowers are fragrant. The leaves are long, narrow, pointed and finely toothed. The adhesion to the pit, whether it clings (clingstone) and whether it separates freely (freestone) is an important characteristic.

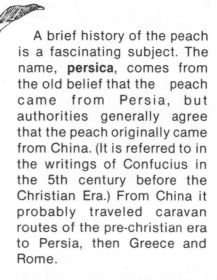

A brief history of the peach is a fascinating subject. The name, **persica**, comes from the old belief that the peach came from Persia, but authorities generally agree that the peach originally came from China. (It is referred to in the writings of Confucius in the 5th century before the Christian Era.) From China it probably traveled caravan routes of the pre-christian era to Persia, then Greece and Rome.

The peach came to America within a few years after the landing of the pilgrims (1620). Peach stones were among the seeds ordered by the Governor for the Massachusetts Bay Colony in New England in 1629. The planting of peach orchards for home use in different parts of the United States was common by the close of the 1700 s, and commercial peach growing appears to have developed after the Civil War. In the beginning of the commercial peach growing, much of the peach production was used to make peach brandy. Today the bulk of the peach crop is used in the fresh state.

Reports of peaches growing in South Carolina are recorded by William Sayle who led the colony that settled at Charleston in 1670. Other reports dated 1700, 1850, and so on are recorded. The commercial production of peaches in South Carolina dates from 1860. The South Carolina Peach Growers Association was organized in 1924 as a result of the realization of the importance of marketing the peach production.

The present-day peach industry in Georgia grew out of home orchards on the famous Georgia plantations. With the introduction of the Elberta variety with its large size, great beauty, and keeping qualities which outclassed all other varieties to date, Georgia and the peach industry became history.

The "Peach Era" in New England began about 1890 and at the turn of the century, Connecticut was one of the largest peach-producing states in the nation. In late December, 1917, New England experienced a "severe cold spell" bringing the "Peach Era" in New England to an abrupt end. (This information came from John Lyman, Sr., whose father, Charles E. Lyman, was an enthusiastic peach grower in Connecticut during the "Peach Era.")

America produces one-fourth of the total world peach supply. Statistics show that California, South Carolina and Georgia are the three leading states in the production of peaches.

The Pick of the Crop

Check the fragrance of the peach; does it have that special "peachy" aroma? Fragrance is an indicator of ripeness. Look at the color; does it have a creamy gold to yellow background with no hint of green? Creamy to gold undercolor also indicates the ripeness of the peach. Red color is not always a sign of ripeness; the red blush of a peach indicates variety and not necessarily ripeness. Look for a well-defined crease in all varieties. Firmness is also important, but as you check for firmness, do not pinch or squeeze but gently place in the palm of your hand and apply pressure. Many fresh peaches have to be picked "firm ripe" so they won't bruise in shipping. These peaches which are bought firm-ripe may be ripened on a counter out of direct sunlight in a ripening bowl or a bag which has a few holes in it to allow some air circulation.

Nutritionists agree that much of the full, deep flavor and nutrients in the peach are found in the skin. Peach skin adds roughage and fiber to your diet, so, when the recipe allows, save time, save flavor, save vitamins and minerals, save money and don't peel peaches! But, when you must peel, here's an easy way to peel peaches. Cover with boiling water, let stand about a minute; strip off the skins.

Peaches are customarily classified in two general categories, freestone and clingstone. A freestone peach is just what the name implies; the fruit parts readily from the stone or pit. The clingstone is a more solid fruit and is more difficult to separate from the pit. Freestones are most popular for home canning, table and general use; clingstones are primarily for commercial use.

There are hundreds of varieties of peaches, and like other fruit, different varieties are used in different ways. For general purposes we can place varieties into early, mid-season and late season groupings. All varieties are good for eating out of hand. The mid and late season varieties are best suited for cooking, canning and preserving.

Peaches are a versatile fruit just right for any occasion. They not only are a great way to balance your budget, but they also balance your diet. For nutrition, attractiveness, economy, and taste, peaches are one of nature's more perfect fruits. So, let's buy them, eat them, cook them, preserve them, can them, and freeze them,—all with the helps found in "The Peach Sampler."

Peach Preservation

Preserving is a small investment in the future. Selecting good-quality peaches is the first step to successful results. If picked too green, they won't ripen satisfactorily. The best ripe peaches have a creamy or yellow background. Look for a well-defined crease in all varieties. Fragrance is also an indicator of ripeness. Peaches should ripen on the tree—their flavor and sweetness will not develop during storage. Always select ripe, firm textured peaches, which will have a better flavor and color. Peaches discolor easily so a commercial anti-oxidant should be used to prevent discoloration. (Follow directions on package for proper proportions.) Prepare fruit carefully, working with small quantities at a time. Freestones are most popular for home preserving. There are many books and instructional pamphlets on the market and one of these should be obtained and followed carefully for best results. The Agricultural Extension Service in your state is a good resource for current, up-to-date information. The Home Economist in the Extension Office in your locality can provide you with research-based, reliable information.

Canning Peaches

Canning is one of the easiest and most satisfying ways to ensure having peaches long after the growing season is over. Besides the convenience and eating enjoyment of having home-canned peaches, there is a sense of personal satisfaction. One bushel of fresh peaches equals 48 pounds, which will yield 16-24 quarts canned. (Information on jelly-making is found in that section of recipes.)

Freezing Peaches

Peaches can be frozen successfully. When prepared properly, peaches retain fresh flavor, bright natural color, and nutritive value. The texture may be softer than fresh fruit because the cells break down during freezing. Be familiar with the types of containers available for freezing; usually rigid containers are best. Keep peaches from floating above the syrup by placing crumpled parchment paper, crushed plastic wrap, or waxed paper atop fruit in the container. Peaches may be frozen in a sugar syrup, in sugar, or without any sugar at all. It takes about 1 to 1½ pounds of peaches to yield 1 pint frozen. Additionally, puree* the peaches, sweeten to taste and freeze in small quantities to be used later.

Drying Peaches

Preserving peaches by drying is useful, convenient, inexpensive and requires less storage space. Basically, drying a peach preserves it by removing sufficient moisture to prevent its decay (peaches have an 89 percent water content). Drying requires a method of heating the food to evaporate the moisture and removing the water vapor formed. The packaging and storing of dried peaches is as important as properly reconstituting the dried peaches. Clingstone peaches are best for drying. Dried peaches make an ideal snack for activities such as backpacking and camping because refrigeration is not needed, they are low in bulk and weight, and they provide quick energy. Directions to cook dried peaches are as follows: Rinse fruit and cover with water 1 inch above fruit in saucepan. Cover and simmer gently for 30 to 35 minutes. If desired, add 3 to 4 tablespoons sugar per cup uncooked dried fruit for last 5 minutes of cooking.

Leathering Peaches

Peach leather is the result of drying pureed* peaches. It can be made from fresh, frozen or canned peaches. After pureeing, pour onto a flat surface and dry slowly. When dry, the peaches have a leather-like texture and appearance and can be easily removed from the drying surface (roll while warm). The leather can be varied by adding spices, garnishes or fillings. An economical suggestion: use the pulp left from homemade juice or jelly. In recent years peach leather, as well as other fruit leathers, has been made commercially and can be purchased in the produce or candy section of the local supermarket. Peach leather made at home is free of preservatives. For a snack that is nourishing, appealing to all ages, and inexpensive, fruit leather is a natural treat, requires no refrigeration and makes an ideal bag-lunch snack.

*Puree—a mixture made by pressing peaches through a sieve or food mill, or by whirling them in a blender so that they are smooth and thick. The puree is used as is in leathers, on ice creams, as a topping, frozen for later use, etc. The word is French, derived from the medieval French "purer" meaning to cleanse, which indicates that originally to puree foods meant to remove their impurities.

Easy Baking Tips

READ the recipe·
GATHER ingredients·
ROUND-UP utensils·
MEASURE ACCURATELY·
FOLLOW directions·
USE size pan recommended·
PRE-HEAT oven unless otherwise stated.

Use standardized measuring cups and spoons. There are two kinds of measuring cups—dry and liquid. Dry measuring cups are made straight across the top so that ingredients can be "leveled off." Liquid measuring cups are usually "see through" and should have a rim above the one-cup line. Liquid measuring cups also have an extended lip which makes pouring easier. They can usually be found in 1-cup, 2-cup, and 1-quart sizes. Measuring spoons come in sets with ¼ teaspoon, ½ teaspoon, 1 teaspoon and 1 tablespoon sizes.

Brown Sugar—always pack firmly in cup to measure.

Butter—do not use **WHIPPED** butter or margarine as a substitute for butter or margarine as the volume is not the same.

Flour—sift before measuring if recipe calls for sifted flour. Use all-purpose flour unless otherwise specified.

Shortening—measure by packing firmly in a graduated measuring cup to the top.

An easy way to crush peaches (and no need to peel them first): a small can (like a juice concentrate can) with both ends cut out, a pastry blender, or mesh-type potato masher, or, of course, the electric blender.

Abbreviations and Symbols

Teaspoon	tsp
Tablespoon	T
Cup	c
Package	pkg
Ounce	oz
Pound	lb
Medium	md
Large	lg
Small	sm
Dozen	dz
Pint	pt
Quart	qt
Carton	ctn
Bottle	btl

Measurements
3 teaspoons = 1 tablespoon
2 tablespoons = 1/8 cup
4 tablespoons = ¼ cup
5 tablespoons + 1 teaspoon = ⅓ cup
8 tablespoons = ½ cup
10 tablespoons + 2 teaspoons = ⅔ cup
12 tablespoons = ¾ cup
14 tablespoons = 7/8 cup
16 tablespoons = 1 cup
2 cups = 1 pint
2 pints = 1 quart
4 quarts = 1 gallon
8 quarts = 1 peck
4 pecks = 1 bushel
1 bushel = 50 pounds = 32-48 pints
1 oz = 2 tablespoons
4 oz = ½ cup
8 oz = 1 cup
16 oz = 1 pound
2 cups granulated sugar = 1 pound
2 ⅔ cups powdered sugar = 1 pound
2 ⅔ cups brown sugar = 1 pound
4 cups sifted flour = 1 pound
2 cups or 4 sticks butter = pound

Contents of cans:

Size	Average contents	Weight
#300	1¾ cups	14-16 oz
#1 tall	2 cups	16-17 oz
# 303	2 cups	16-17 oz
# 2	2½ cups	20 oz
# 2½	3½ cups	27-29 oz
# 3	5¾ cups	46 oz
# 10	12-13 cups	6½ lbs

If the recipe calls for a can size that has changed, get the can in nearest weight.

Commercially canned foods are considered safe because they are processed under carefully controlled conditions. However, if a canned food shows any signs of spoilage, do not use it. Do not even taste it. Signs to be wary of: bulging can ends, leakage, spurting liquid, off-odor or mold.

Oven Temperatures:

Slow oven	250-325 degrees
Moderate oven	350-375 degrees
Hot oven	400-450 degrees
Very Hot oven	450-500 degrees

Word Glossary

Aspic — a savory jelly of meat juice, tomato juice, or fruit juice.

Bavarian — pudding made with a gelatin-cream base.

Bombe — a frozen dessert of two or more mixtures packed into a melon-shaped mold.

Blintz — a thin pancake or crepe filled and rolled, usually with a cream cheese or cottage cheese filling.

Compote — a mixture of sweetened fruits.

Condiment — sauces and relishes to add to food at the table to enhance the flavor.

Cobbler — a deep dish fruit pie made with a rich pastry or biscuit dough top.

Crêpe — a very small thin pancake

Frappé — a mushy frozen fruit dessert.

Fondue — a dip usually of melted cheese.

Gourmet — a connoisseur of fine food.

Ice — a frozen mixture of fruit juice or fruit puree and a sweetener mixed with water.

Kuchen — a cake, often coffeecake.

Mousse — a frozen refreshment made of fruits or flavorings folded into sweetened whipped cream or thin cream and gelatin, then frozen in a mold without stirring.

Macédoine — a mixture of fruits or vegetables.

Meringue — a stiffly beaten mixture of sugar and egg white used as a pie topping or baked and served as a dessert shell.

Puree — to reduce food to a smooth, velvety medium by whirling in an electric blender or pressing through a sieve.

Parfait — ice cream, fruit and whipped cream layered dessert.

Sherbet — a fruit juice, sugar, egg white and milk or water mixture which is frozen.

Torte — a rich cake, variously made.

by Eliza Mears Horton

The Peach Sampler

Helpful Information

One pound of fresh peaches will equal:
- 3-4 medium sized peaches   OR
- 2 cups sliced peaches   OR
- 1½ cups pulp or puree   OR
- 4 servings.

Two pounds of peaches makes 1 nine-inch pie.

A 10-ounce package of frozen peaches = 3 (½ cup) servings.

Calorie Count:
- Peaches, canned with syrup — 2 halves = 75
- Peaches, fresh — 1 medium = 38
- Peaches, frozen — 4 ounce = 89

Nutritional Information (1 medium peach):

Calories	38
Protein	0.6 grams
Fat	0.1 grams
Carbohydrates	9.7 grams
Calcium	9 milligrams
Iron	0.5 milligrams
Vitamin A	1300 I.U.
Thiamin B	0.02 milligrams
Riboflavin B 2	0.05 milligrams
Niacin	1.0 milligrams
Vitamin C	7 mIligrams

When peaches are cut or peeled, keep their color bright by treating them with ascorbic acid, commercial color keeper or a citrus juice. Pure ascorbic acid may be found in crystalline and powdered forms and usually is available at your local pharmacy. Commercial color keeper preparations are not pure ascorbic acid, but rather a mixture of ascorbic acid and sugar. Use the commercial brand of your choice and follow directions on the package. There are several on the market and usually available in your supermarket.

Pastries

Everyone wants a "piece of the pie"—or cake—or cobbler. Pastries are the all-time favorite American dessert. The aroma of fresh-baked pastries conjures up images of very special edibles. Cookies, small pastries, and tarts, small enough to handle easily but large enough to satisfy, are favorites with anyone who enjoys finger-tip sweets. Bread-making is a very special art and peach breads can be made during peach season and frozen for winter enjoyment. On special occasions of every kind, the center of attraction is very often a cake. Bake a pie, a turnover, or even a peach pizza?! and get ready for the compliments.

PASTRY SHELLS

1. Basic Pie Pastry (for single crust)
Sift together 1½ cups sifted all-purpose flour and ½ teaspoon salt; cut in ½ cup shortening with pastry blender or blending fork till pieces are the size of small peas. Sprinkle 1 tablespoon cold water over part of mixture. Gently toss with fork; push to side of bowl. Sprinkle next tablespoon water over dry part, mix lightly; push to moistened part at side. Repeat till 4 to 5 tablespoons cold water has been used and all dry ingredients are moistened. Form into ball. Flatten ball on lightly floured surface. Roll from center to edge till dough is 1/8 inch thick. Fit pastry into pie plate, trim ½ to 1 inch beyond edge; fold under and flute.

2. Oil Pastry (makes two single crusts or 1 double crust)
Sift together 2 cups all-purpose flour and 1½ teaspoons salt. Pour ½ cup salad oil and 4 to 5 tablespoons cold water (or milk) into measuring cup (do not stir). Add all at once to flour mixture. Stir lightly with fork. Form into 2 balls; flatten slightly. Roll each between two 12-inch squares of waxed paper. When dough is rolled to edges of paper, it will be right thickness for crust. Peel off top sheet of paper and fit dough, paper side up into pie plate. Remove paper. For single crust, trim ½ to 1 inch beyond edge; fold under and flute. For baked pie crust, prick bottom and sides well with fork. Bake at 450° for 10 to 12 minutes. For double crust, trim lower crust with rim of pie plate. Cut slits in upper crust. Fit loosely over filling; trim ½ inch beyond edge; tuck under edge of lower crust. Flute.

3. Pecan Crust (makes 2 crusts)
Prepare 1 package pie crust mix as package directs. Divide in half and roll out on lightly floured board into two 8-inch circles. Sprinkle each circle with ½ cup finely chopped pecans evenly over surface. Continue to roll out to fit 9-inch pie plate. Crimp edges. Prick with fork. Bake at 425° for 12 to 15 minutes or until golden. Cool.

4. Graham Cracker Crust
Combine 1¼ cups graham cracker crumbs and 3 tablespoons sugar in medium-sized bowl. Stir in 6 tablespoons melted butter or margarine until thoroughly blended. Pack mixture firmly into 9-inch pie pan and press firmly to bottom and sides, bringing crumbs evenly up to rim. Chill one hour before filling OR bake at 350° for 8 minutes. Cook, chill and till.

5. Vanilla Wafer Crust
Mix together 1½ cups fine vanilla wafer crumbs and 6 tablespoons melted butter or margarine. Press firmly into a 9-inch pie plate. Chill.

6. Gingersnap-Graham Crust

In mixing bowl toss together ¾ cup fine gingersnap crumbs, ½ cup fine graham cracker crumbs, ¼ cup melted butter or margarine and 2 tablespoons sugar. Turn crumb mixture into a 9-inch pie plate. Spread the crumb mixture evenly in the pie plate. Press onto bottom and sides to form a firm, even crust. Bake at 375° for 4 to 5 minutes. Cool thoroughly on rack.

7. Meringue Crust

In mixer bowl beat together 2 egg whites, ½ teaspoon vanilla, ¼ teaspoon **each** salt and cream of tartar. Gradually add ½ cup sugar and beat to stiff peaks and till sugar is dissolved. Fold in ½ cup chopped pecans. Spread mixture onto bottom and sides of well-buttered 9-inch pie plate, building up the sides with a spoon to form a shell. Bake at 275° for 1 hour. Turn off heat and let dry in oven with door closed 1 hour more. Cool on rack.

PRETTY PEACH MERINGUE PIE   275° — 1¼ Hours

8		egg whites
½	tsp	EACH cream of tartar and salt
1⅓	c	EACH granulated sugar and sifted powdered sugar
1	tsp	vanilla extract
1	pkg	(3¼ oz) vanilla pudding and pie filling
¼	tsp	almond extract
1½	c	sliced peaches
¼	c	blueberries

Have egg whites at room temperature. Beat at moderate speed until foamy. Add cream of tartar and salt and beat to distribute. Turn mixer to moderately high speed and add granulated sugar very gradually. Then add powdered sugar gradually. Stop mixer and scrape bowl so that no undissolved sugar remains around the edge of bowl. Add vanilla. Continue beating until mixture is thick and satiny and stands in stiff peaks, about 20 minutes. Mark a 9-inch circle on unglazed brown paper; put on cookie sheet. Spread some of merginue on brown paper within circle to form a base about ¾ inch thick. Put remaining meringue around edge of circle with a pastry bag and tube or with a spoon. Bake at 275° for 1¼ hours. Turn off heat and leave in oven for 1 more hour. Remove paper and cool on rack. Prepare pudding according to package directions, flavor with almond extract and chill. Use to fill meringue. Top with peaches and sprinkle with blueberries.

Makes 10 to 12 servings.

FRESH PEACH MERINGUE   400°

6		egg whites
¼	tsp	salt
½	tsp	cream of tartar
1¾	c	sugar
1½	tsp	vanilla
6		fresh peaches
2	T	lemon juice
1	env	(1T) unflavored gelatin
2	T	cold water
		Vanilla Whipped Cream

Place the egg whites, salt and cream of tartar in large mixer bowl and beat with electric mixer until egg whites have doubled in volume. Beat in 1½ **cups** sugar, **1 tablespoon at a time,** being sure each addition of sugar is dissolved before adding the next. Beat in vanilla and spoon into a buttered 8-inch springform pan. Make a depression in center about 5 inches wide and 1 inch deep with the back of a tablespoon. Place in preheated oven, close door and turn off heat. Leave meringue in oven for 12 hours or overnight without opening oven door. Remove from oven and run a spatula around sides to loosen from pan. Release the spring and gently lift off sides of pan. Slide meringue off pan onto a serving plate carefully. Peel and slice peaches and place in a bowl. Sprinkle with lemon juice and remaining ¼ cup sugar. Soften gelatin in cold water and dissolve over hot water. Blend with peach mixture and chill until thickened. Pile into meringue and top with Vanilla Whipped-Cream: Whip ½ cup whipping cream, 1 tablespoon sugar, and ¼ teaspoon vanilla until stiff and fold in sugar and vanilla. Garnish with peaches and serve at once.

THE BEST PEACH CHIFFON PIE

3	c	sliced fresh peaches
½	c	sugar
1	env	unflavored gelatin
1¼	c	cold water
½	c	whipping cream, whipped
1		9-inch baked pastry shell

Sprinkle peaches with sugar and set aside. Soften gelatin in cold water; dissolve over low heat; cool. Drain syrup from peaches; stir syrup into gelatin mixture. Chill till partially set; beat till fluffy. Fold in peaches and whipped cream. Pile into pastry shell and chill.

VERY GOOD PEACH CHIFFON PIE

1		baked pastry shell
1	can	(29 oz) peach halves
¼	c	sugar
1	env	(1 T) unflavored gelatin
¼	tsp	salt
½	tsp	finely shredded lemon peel
2	T	lemon juice
3		egg yolks, slightly beaten
3		egg whites
⅓	c	sugar
		Unsweetened whipped cream, optional

Drain canned peach halves, reserving ½ cup peach syrup and 1 peach half. Place the remaining peach halves in a blender container. Cover and blend just till peaches are pureed; set aside. In saucepan combine ¼ cup sugar, unflavored gelatin and salt. Stir in the ½ cup reserved syrup, finely shredded lemon peel, lemon juice and egg yolks. Cook, stirring constantly, till gelatin is dissolved and mixture is slightly thickened and bubbly. Add the pureed peaches. Chill gelatin mixture to the consistency of corn syrup, stirring occasionally. Immediately beat egg whites till soft peaks form. Gradually add ⅓ cup sugar, beating till stiff peaks form. When gelatin is the consistency of unbeaten egg whites (partially set), fold in stiff-beaten egg whites. Chill till mixture mounds when spooned. Turn into baked pastry shell. Chill several hours or overnight till set. To serve, slice the reserved peach half. Garnish chilled pie with the peach slices. Top with dollops of unsweetened whipped cream, if desired.

FANCIFUL PEACH CHIFFON PIE

¾	c	sugar
2½	T	cornstarch
¾	c	water
3	T	peach flavored gelatin
		Few drops almond extract
3	c	sliced ripe fresh peaches
1	T	lemon juice
1		9-inch baked pie shell
½	pt	whipping cream, whipped

Combine sugar, cornstarch and water in a saucepan and cook over medium heat until thickened. Add gelatin and almond extract and cool. Slice peaches and sprinkle with lemon juice; fold into the cooled gelatin mixture; pour into the pie shells. Cover with whipped cream and chill. Serve cold.

INCREDIBLE PEACH PIE   350° — 40-50 Minute

2		eggs
½	c	whole milk
½	c	light corn syrup
¼	c	butter or margarine, melted
¼	c	sugar
1	tsp	vanilla
½	c	SELF-RISING flour
1	c	coconut
2½	c	chopped peaches
½	c	chopped pecans
		Nutmeg or cinnamon

In a large bowl, beat the eggs and add milk, corn syrup, butter, sugar, vanilla and flour. Mix until smooth. Stir in coconut and peaches. Pour into greased and floured 10-inch pie plate. Top peach mixture with chopped pecans and sprinkle generously with nutmeg or cinnamon. Bake at 350° for 40-50 minutes or until the custard is set. Allow to stand 15-30 minutes for easier serving. Refrigerate any leftovers.

Makes 6 to 8 servings.

Georgia Peach Commission

EASY PEACH CUSTARD PIE   375° — 15 Minutes
                                      + 30-35 Minutes

1	c	all-purpose flour
2	T	sugar
¼	tsp	salt
½	tsp	baking powder
¼	c	margarine
2	c	sliced peaches
⅓	c	sugar
1	tsp	cinnamon
1		egg
1	c	whipping cream or half-and-half

Mix together flour, sugar, salt and baking powder. Cut in margarine until mixture is crumbly. Press into the bottom and half way up the sides of a 10-inch pie plate. Arrange sliced peaches in over-lapping rows of rings. Mix sugar and cinnamon and sprinkle over the peaches. Bake at 375° for 15 minutes. Meanwhile mix egg and cream thoroughly. Pour over peaches and return to the oven for 30-35 minutes or until the custard is set and lightly browned. Serve warm.

Makes 8 servings.

Georgia Peach Commission

PINEAPPLE PEACH CUSTARD PIE   450° — 5 Minutes

Pastry for single crust pie: Line a 9-inch pie plate, trim pastry to ½-inch beyond edge of pie plate. Flute edge; do not prick pastry. Bake at 450° for 5 minutes. Cool thoroughly.

375° — 15 Minutes + 15-20 Minutes

1	can	(21 oz) peach pie filling
1	can	(8¼ oz) crushed pineapple, drained
1	c	dairy sour cream
1	pkg	(3 oz) cream cheese, softened
2		eggs
⅓	c	sugar

In mixing bowl combine pie filling and crushed pineapple; turn into the partially baked pastry shell. In mixer bowl with electric mixer or rotary beater, beat together sour cream and cream cheese; add eggs and sugar, beating mixture till smooth. Place pie shell on oven rack; pour sour cream-egg mixture over peach-pineapple layer. To prevent overbrowning, cover edge of pie with foil. Bake at 375° for 15 minutes. Remove foil; bake for 15 to 20 minutes more or till crust is golden and filling is set. Cool on rack. Cover, chill to store.

EXCELLENT PEACH CUSTARD PIE   450° — 5 Minutes

Pastry for single crust pie:

Line a 9-inch pie plate, trim pastry to ½-inch beyond edge of pie plate. Flute edge; do not prick pastry. Bake at 450° for 5 minutes. Cool thoroughly.

350° — 25 Minutes + 20-25 Minutes

3	c	fresh or frozen sliced peaches
2/3	c	sugar
2	T	all-purpose flour
¼	tsp	salt
2		eggs, slightly beaten
1	c	light cream or whole milk
		Ground nutmeg

Thaw and drain frozen peaches OR thinly sliced fresh peaches. Place sliced peaches in bottom of partially baked pastry shell. In mixing bowl combine sugar, flour and salt; stir in eggs. Stir in cream or milk. Place pie shell on oven rack. Carefully pour filling over peaches. Sprinkle a little nutmeg atop. To prevent overbrowning cover edge of pie with foil. Bake at 350° for 25 minutes. Remove foil; bake for 20 to 25 minutes more or till knife inserted off-center comes out clean. Cool on rack before serving. Cover; chill to store.

GOLDEN-FRIED PEACH PIES

1½	c	SELF-RISING flour
4	T	shortening
4-5	T	water
1	can	(16 oz) peaches
½	T	cinnamon
1	T	melted butter

Sift the flour into a bowl and cut in shortening. Add enough water gradually to hold pastry together and press into a ball. Divide into 5 parts and roll each part on a floured surface into a 5-inch circle. Drain the peaches and mash. Add the cinnamon and butter and mix well. Place 2 tablespoons peach mixture on each circle and fold over. Seal edges with a wet fork. Fry in deep fat at 375° until golden brown and drain on absorbent paper.

FRESH PEACH FRIED PIES

3	T	cornstarch
¾	c	sugar
		Pinch of salt
¾	c	water
3		fresh peaches, peeled and diced fine
¼	tsp	almond flavoring, optional
2	cans	dairy-case canned biscuits
		Vegetable cooking oil

Mix cornstarch, sugar, salt and water in a small saucepan until thoroughly dissolved. Cook over low heat stirring constantly until thick and clear. Add diced peaches and flavoring and set aside while preparing pastry. On a lightly floured board roll each individual biscuit very thin. Set aside and let rise (about 10 minutes). After the dough has risen, roll each biscuit very thin again. Spread filling of thickened fresh peaches over half of each biscuit. Fold dough over and press edges together very carefully so that filling is sealed inside the biscuit. (Edges can be crimped together with fork.) Heat oil in an electric skillet or on top of range to 360°. Place individual pies in hot oil and fry to desired brownness. Turn only once to brown sides. Drain on paper towel. Serve warm.

Yield: 20 pies.

South Carolina Department of Agriculture

HOMEMADE FRIED PEACH PIES

2	c	all-purpose flour
1	tsp	salt
½	c	butter or shortening
⅓	c	cold water
		Mashed sweetened peaches

Sift flour and salt together, cut in the butter and mix with hands. Add water. Roll about 1/8-inch thick (between wax paper if butter is used) on floured board. Cut with large cookie cutter about 4 inches in diameter. In each round, place 1½ tablespoons mashed peaches. Moisten edges with water, fold to make a semicircle and press edges together with a fork. Fry in deep fat.

S.C. Department of Agriculture

CRANBERRY-PEACH PIE

375° — 20 Minutes
+ 20-25 Minutes

A Holiday Winner!

1	can	(29 oz) peach slices
3	c	fresh cranberries
1½	c	sugar
3	T	cornstarch
¼	c	chopped toasted almonds
		Pastry for double-crust pie

Drain peaches, reserving 1 cup syrup; coarsely cut up peaches and set aside. In saucepan combine cranberries and reserved peach syrup; cook 5 to 8 minutes or till skins of cranberries pop. Combine sugar and cornstarch. Stir into hot cranberries. Cook quickly, stirring constantly, till mixture is thickened and bubbly. Remove from heat. Stir in peaches and almonds; set aside to cool. Line a 9-inch pie plate. Pour peach mixture into pastry-lined pie plate. Cut remaining pastry into ½-inch-wide strips. Weave strips atop filling to make lattice crust; flute edge. To prevent overbrowning, cover edge of pie with foil. Bake at 375° for 20 minutes. Remove foil; bake for 20 to 25 minutes more. Cool on rack before serving.

GOLDEN PEACH PIE   400° — 40-45 Minutes

Notice the subtle flavor of almond and nutmeg.

1	can	(29 oz) sliced peaches
½	c	sugar
2	T	all-purpose flour
¼	tsp	nutmeg
		Dash salt
2	T	butter or margarine
1	T	lemon juice
½	tsp	grated orange peel
1/8	tsp	almond extract
		Pastry for 9-inch lattice-top pie

Drain peaches, reserving ⅓ cup syrup. Combine sugar, flour, nutmeg and salt; add reserved syrup. Cook and stir till mixture thickens. Add next 4 ingredients, then peaches. Line 9-inch pie plate with pastry; fill with peach mixture. Adjust lattice top; seal. Sprinkle with sugar. Bake at 400° for 40-45 minutes. If pie browns too quickly, cover edge with foil. Serve warm.

BROWN SUGAR PEACH PIE   400° — 35 Minutes

The Caramel Sauce makes the difference!

		Pastry for 9-inch lattice-top pie
¾	c	brown sugar
⅓	c	all-purpose flour
3	T	light corn syrup
1	T	lemon juice
⅓	c	softened butter or margarine
6		fresh peaches, sliced
	OR	
1	can	(29 oz) sliced peaches

Combine brown sugar, flour, corn syrup, lemon juice and butter. Cook and stir over low heat till sugar is dissolved; cool slightly. Arrange sliced peaches in pastry-lined 9-inch pie plate; pour brown sugar mixture over. Adjust lattice crust; seal. Bake at 400° for 35 minutes. Cool before serving.

ORANGE-PEACH PIE

375° — 30 Minutes
+ 30-40 Minutes

		Pastry for double-crust pie
¾	c	sugar
1	tsp	finely shredded orange peel
2	T	all-purpose flour
4	c	sliced fresh peaches
2	lg	oranges, peeled and sectioned, and cut-up
2	T	butter or margarine

In mixing bowl stir together sugar, orange peel and flour; blend in peaches and oranges. Turn into pastry-lined pie plate. Dot with butter. Cut remaining pastry into ½-inch-wide strips. Weave strips atop filling to make lattice crust; flute edge. To prevent overbrowning, cover edge of pie with foil. Bake at 375° for 30 minutes. Remove foil; bake for 30 to 40 minutes more. Cool.

Whatever is worth doing at all is worth doing well.

Chesterfield

GLORIOUS DEEP-DISH PEACH PIE

375° — 25 Minutes
+ 30-35 Minutes

¾	c	sugar
3	T	all-purpose flour
¼	tsp	ground nutmeg
6	c	fresh peeled, thickly sliced peaches
3	T	grenadine syrup
3	T	lemon juice
2	T	butter or margarine
		Pastry for single-crust pie

In large bowl combine sugar, flour and nutmeg; add peaches and toss till well-coated. Let mixture stand 5 minutes. Carefully stir in grenadine and lemon juice. Turn mixture into a 1½-quart casserole or a 10-inch round deep baking dish, spreading peaches evenly; dot with butter. Prepare and roll out pastry to fit size of dish, flute to sides of dish but not over edge. To prevent overbrowning, cover edge with foil. Place dish on bakingsheet in oven. Bake at 375° for 25 minutes. Remove foil; bake for 30 to 35 minutes more or till crust is golden.

DEEP DISH ORANGE PEACH PIE

400° — 40 Minutes

¾	c	sugar
3	T	all-purpose flour
1	tsp	grated orange peel
		Dash nutmeg
2	c	orange sections, cut up
1	can	(29 oz) sliced peaches, drained
2	T	butter or margarine
1		unbaked pie crust for top

Combine sugar, flour, orange peel and nutmeg. Mix with orange sections and sliced peaches. Turn into 8x8x2-inch baking dish. Dot with butter or margarine. Place unbaked pie crust atop filling, cutting slits for escape of steam. Crimp to edges of baking dish. Bake at 400° for about 40 minutes. Serve warm; top with ice cream.

MARVELOUS DEEP-DISH PEACH PIE

425° — 40 Minutes

½	c	brown sugar, firmly packed
3	T	cornstarch
¼	tsp	salt
½	c	light corn syrup
5	c	peeled, sliced peaches
2	T	margarine
		Pastry for top crust.

In large bowl mix together sugar, cornstarch and salt. Stir in corn syrup. Add peaches; toss to coat well. Turn into a 10x6x2-inch baking dish or 1½-quart casserole. Dot with margarine. On lightly floured surface roll out pastry ¼ inch larger in each direction than baking dish. Cut slits to allow steam to escape. Place pastry over peaches. Seal and flute edge. Bake at 425° for 40 minutes or until crust is brown.
Makes 6 servings.

MINCEMEAT-PEACH PIE   425° — 30-35 Minutes

1	pkg	(9 oz) dry mincemeat
½	c	water
1	can	(16 oz) peach pie filling
1	T	grated orange rind, divided
		Pastry for double-crust 9-inch pie
2	tsp	half-and-half
1	T	sugar

Combine mincemeat and water in a saucepan; bring to a boil and boil 1 minute. Remove from heat; stir in pie filling and **2 teaspoons** orange rind. Pour into a pastry-lined 9-inch pie plate; top with remaining pastry. Trim edges; then seal and flute. Cut slits in crust for steam to escape. Brush with half-and-half. Combine remaining orange rind and sugar; sprinkle over pastry. Bake at 425° for 30-35 minutes or until browned.

Yield: one 9-inch pie.

GOLD CREST PIE

1		baked pie shell, cooled
1	can	(16 oz) peach slices
1½	c	mincemeat
¼	c	sugar
1½	T	cornstarch
1	tsp	grated lemon rind
½	c	whipping cream
1	tsp	brown sugar
½	tsp	pumpkin pie spice

Drain syrup from peaches into saucepan and reserve 6 to 8 peach slices for garnish. Chop remaining peach slices and add to the syrup. Add the mincemeat, sugar, cornstarch and lemon rind and mix well. Bring to a boil over medium heat, stirring constantly, and cook until thickened and clear. Turn into pie shell and cool thoroughly. Whip the cream until stiff and fold in brown sugar and spice. Spoon over pie in wide border and garnish with reserved peach slices.

MINCE-PEACH PIE

375° — 25 Minutes
+ 25 Minutes

Pastry for double-crust pie
1   jar   (28 oz) prepared mincemeat
1   can   (29 oz) sliced peaches, drained
Milk and sugar

In mixing bowl combine prepared mincemeat and drained peaches. Pour mixture into pastry-lined pie plate. Cut slits in top crust; place pastry atop filling. Seal and flute edge. Brush top with a little milk and sprinkle with some sugar. To prevent overbrowning, cover edge of pie with foil. Bake at 375° for 25 minutes. Remove foil; bake about 25 minutes more or till crust is golden. Cool on rack before serving.

LUSCIOUS PEACH PIE

2   pkgs (3 oz each) cream cheese, softened
¾   c   sifted powdered sugar
¼   tsp   almond extract
¾   c   whipping cream, whipped
1   can   (16 oz) sliced peaches, drained
1   graham cracker crust (9-inch)

Combine cream cheese, powdered sugar, and almond extract; beat until smooth. Fold in whipped cream and gently stir in peaches. Pour filling into graham cracker crust. Chill well.

PEACH REVEL PIE

About 20 vanilla wafers
1   qt   peach or vanilla ice cream, softened
1   c   fresh peach sauce*
¼   c   nuts or coconut

Line bottom and sides of 9-inch pie pan with wafers, round sides to bottom and edge of pan. Spread half of ice cream over wafers. Top with **half** of sauce. Repeat with rest of ice cream and sauce. Sprinkle with nuts or coconut. Freeze. Keep frozen until about 25 minutes before serving.

*Fresh Peach Sauce: Combine 2 cups crushed fresh peaches, ½ cup sugar, ½ cup orange juice in 1½-quart pan. Stir over high heat until boiling. Simmer, uncovered, about 15 minutes or until thick. Remove from heat. Stir in 2 teaspoons lemon juice and 1 teaspoon vanilla. Cool. Yield: 2 cups.

S.C. Department of Agriculture

FRESH PEACH PIE

1		9-inch baked pastry shell
2	c	fresh sliced peaches
1	c	mashed peaches
½	c	orange juice
1	c	sugar
2½	T	cornstarch

Fill pastry shell with 2 cups fresh sliced peaches. In a saucepan, boil mashed peaches, orange juice, sugar and cornstarch until mixture is clear (stirring constantly) and slightly thickened. Pour heated mixture over peaches in pie shell. Cool thoroughly before serving.

S.C. Department of Agriculture

Nature imitates herself. A grain thrown into good ground brings forth fruit; a principle thrown into a good mind brings forth fruit. Everything is created and conducted by the same Master: the root, the branch, the fruits - the principles, the consequences.

Blaise Pascal

FROZEN PEACH MELBA PIE

1	lb	fresh peeled, sliced peaches
¾	c	light corn syrup
1	T	lemon juice
2		drops red food color, optional
1	pt	raspberry sherbet, softened
2		drops yellow food color, optional
1	c	vanilla ice cream, softened
1		9-inch graham cracker crust
		Peach slices

In blender container place peaches, corn syrup and lemon juice; cover. Blend 30 seconds or until pureed. Fold **1 cup** of the pureed peaches and red food color into raspberry sherbet. Pour into crust. Freeze about 1 hour or until firm. Fold remaining pureed peaches and yellow food color into vanilla ice cream. Pour over raspberry layer. Cover; freeze until firm. If desired, garnish with peach slices.

Georgia Peach Commission

CREAM CHEESE-PEACH PIE

1	pkg	(3 oz) cream cheese
1		baked pastry shell
7		peaches, sliced
1	c	sugar
¼	c	water
2	T	cornstarch
1	tsp	almond flavoring
		Whipped Cream

Soften the cream cheese and spread over pastry shell. Place **5** sliced peaches over cream cheese in pastry shell. Combine the sugar, water, cornstarch and remaining peaches in a saucepan and cook, stirring, until thickened. Cool and add almond flavoring. Pour over peaches in the pastry shell and chill. Top with whipped cream and serve.

Makes 6 to 8 servings.

PEACH PARFAIT PIE

		Gingersnap-Graham Crust*
3½	c	fresh peeled, sliced peaches
¼	c	sugar
1	pkg	(3 oz) lemon-flavored gelatin
1	pt	vanilla ice cream
		Unsweetened whipped cream
		Ground nutmeg

Gingersnap-Graham Crust: In mixing bowl toss together ¾ cup gingersnap crumbs, ½ cup graham cracker crumbs, ¼ cup melted butter or margarine and 2 tablespoons sugar. Turn crumb mixture into a 9-inch pie plate. Spread the crumb mixture evenly in the pie plate. Press onto bottom and sides to form a firm, even crust. Bake at 375° for 4 to 5 minutes. Cool thoroughly on rack.

In mixing bowl combine peaches and sugar; toss gently to coat and set aside for about 15 minutes. Drain peaches, reserving the syrup and 10 peach slices. Add enough water to the reserved syrup to measure 1 cup liquid. Heat fruit liquid to boiling; remove from heat. Add gelatin, stir till gelatin is dissolved. Pour gelatin mixture into large mixing bowl. Add ice cream by spoonfuls, stirring till melted. Chill till mixture mounds when spooned. Fold in sliced peaches. Turn peach mixture into baked crust. Chill pie several hours or overnight till set. Arrange the reserved peach slices spoke-fashion atop pie. Garnish with whipped cream and sprinkle with nutmeg. Cover; chill to store.

RASPBERRY-PEACH PIE

1		9-inch vanilla wafer crust*
1½	c	diced fresh peaches
½	c	fresh or frozen raspberries
½	c	sugar
1	pkg	(3 oz) lemon-flavored gelatin
1	c	boiling water
1/8	tsp	almond extract
		Dash salt
½	c	whipping cream, whipped

*Vanilla Wafer Crust: Mix together 1½ cups fine vanilla wafer crumbs and 6 tablespoons melted butter or margarine. Press firmly into a 9-inch pie plate. Chill.

Combine peaches, raspberries and sugar; let stand 30 minutes. Drain, reserving syrup. Dissolve gelatin in boiling water and cool. Add fruit syrup, extract and salt. Chill till partially set; fold in fruit and whipped cream. Pile into chilled crust. Chill pie several hours or overnight till set. Garnish with fresh mint, if desired. Cover, chill to store.

PEACH PIE UNLIMITED

1		Graham Cracker Crumb Crust*
1	pkg	(3 oz) orange gelatin
2	T	sugar
1	c	boiling water
1	c	cold water
1½	c	sliced peaches

*Graham Cracker Crumb Crust: Combine 1¼ cups graham cracker crumbs and 3 tablespoons sugar in medium-sized bowl. Stir in 6 tablespoons melted butter or margarine until thoroughly blended. Pack mixture firmly into 9-inch pie pan and press firmly to bottom and sides, bringing crumbs evenly up to rim. chill one hour before filling OR bake at 350° for 8 minutes. Cool.

Dissolve gelatin and sugar in boiling water; stir in cold water. Chill until very thick; then fold in peaches. Pour into crumb crust pastry shell. Chill until firm. Garnish with whipped cream or sour cream and additional fruit or sprinkle with nutmeg, if desired.

GEM PEACH PIE

1	pkg	(3 oz) orange gelatin
1	c	boiling water
2	c	ice cubes
½	tsp	almond extract
2	c	peeled, sliced peaches
	OR	
1	can	(16 oz) sliced peaches, drained
1		baked 9-inch pie shell, cooled

Dissolve gelatin in boiling water. Add ice cubes and stir constantly until gelatin starts to thicken - 3 to 5 minutes. Remove any unmelted ice. Add almond extract and peaches. Pour into pie shell. Chill until firm. Garnish with whipped topping and toasted almonds, if desired.

PEACHY ICE CREAM PIE

1		baked Pecan Crust*
2	c	peach puree
2	pkg	(1 oz ea) unflavored gelatin
1	qt	vanilla ice cream, softened slightly
5		fresh peaches, sliced
		Whipped cream

*Pecan Crust: Prepare **one-half** of an 11-ounce package pie crust mix as package directs. Roll out on lightly floured board to 8-inch circle. Sprinkle ½ cup finely chopped pecans evenly over surface. Continue to roll out to fit 9-inch pie plate. Crimp edge. Prick with fork. Bake at 425° for 12 to 15 minutes or until golden. Cool.

Pour 1 cup of the peach puree into small sauce pan; stir in gelatin; dissolve over low heat. Pour mixture into blender; blend smoothly. Gradually add ice cream, blending smoothly. As container gets full, empty part of mixture into bowl. Stir entire mixture thoroughly; chill until mixture mounds, stirring occasionally. Fold sliced peaches into chilled filling, reserving a few slices for garnish. Pour into pie crust. Chill at least 2 hours. Garnish with whipped cream and reserved peach slices.

California Tree Fruit Agreement

Five variations of a dessert you'll love!

POLKA-DOT FRESH PEACH PIE   400° — 45 Minutes

1		unbaked 9-inch pastry crust
6		fresh peaches, peeled and halved
¾	c	sugar
¼	c	flour
½	tsp	mace or cinnamon
1/8	tsp	salt
1	c	whipping cream
¼	c	slivered almonds, optional

Arrange peaches, cut side down in pastry lined pan. Mix sugar, flour, mace and salt. Stir in cream gradually. Pour over peaches. Sprinkle with almonds. Bake at 400° about 45 minutes, until the filling is set. Serve warm or cold.

National Peach Council

CREAM-PEACH PIE   400° — 15 Minutes
                              350° till brown

¾		to 1 c sugar
2	T	flour
		Dash of salt
3		eggs
1-2	c	whole milk or peach juice
1	tsp	almond flavoring
6		to 8 peach halves
1		unbaked pie shell
2	T	butter

Mix sugar, flour, and salt. Beat eggs with liquid and flavoring; add to dry ingredients. Place peach halves, cut-side down, in pie shell. Pour liquid over peaches. Dot with butter. Bake at 400° for 15 minutes; reduce heat to 350° and cook until crust is brown and filling set.

PEACH PIE SUPREME

400° — 10 Minutes
350° — 30-40 Minutes

1		unbaked pastry crust
5		peaches, halved
1	c	sugar
⅓	c	butter or margarine
⅓	c	flour

Arrange peach halves in pastry, cut side up. Mix the sugar, butter and flour until mixture resembles coarse cornmeal and sprinkle over peaches. Bake at 400° for 10 minutes. Reduce temperature to 350° and bake for 30 to 40 minutes longer.

SUMMERTIME PEACH PIE

375°—50-60 Minutes

4	T	cornstarch
1	c	sugar
1		unbaked pie shell
3		medium-sized peaches
1	pt	half & half

Mix cornstarch and sugar together and sprinkle **half** of the mixture into the bottom of an unbaked pie shell. Arrange fresh, peeled peach halves with their cut sides up in the pie shell and sprinkle the rest of the cornstarch and sugar mix over them. Then fill the pie shell with half and half cream until it covers the peaches. Bake at 375° for about 50 to 60 minutes.

Serve with ice cream.

DIVINE DEEP-DISH PEACH PIE

400°

1		unbaked pastry crust
4		peaches, halved
1¼	c	sugar
½	c	brown sugar (packed)
1		stick butter or margarine
3		eggs, beaten

Line a deep pie plate with pastry and place the peaches, cut side up, in pastry. Sprinkle **1 cup sugar** over peaches. Bake at 400° until peaches are tender. Cream remaining sugar, brown sugar and butter in a bowl. Add the eggs and mix well. Pour over peaches and bake until set.

FRESH PEACH PIE

1½	c	sugar
¼	c	cornstarch
	OR	
½	c	all-purpose flour
2	c	water
1	pkg	(3 oz) peach fruit gelatin
4	c	peeled sliced peaches
2		9-inch baked pie shells

Mix sugar and cornstarch. Add water and bring to a boil for 3 minutes; remove from heat. Add package of peach gelatin. **Cool** and add the peaches. Pour into baked and cooled pie shells.

Georgia Peach Commission

GLAZED PEACH PIE

4	c	sliced fresh peaches
¾	c	sugar
1	pkg	(3 oz) orange-flavored gelatin
1	c	boiling water
		Dash of salt
4	tsp	lemon juice
1		baked 9-inch pie shell

Combine fresh peaches and sugar; let stand 10 minutes. Dissolve gelatin in boiling water. Add salt and lemon juice. Cool. Add peaches and chill until slightly thickened. Turn into cold pie shell. Garnish with whipped cream and peach slices.

FRUIT CUP PIE

375° — 25 Minutes
+ 20-25 Minutes

		Pastry for double-crust pie
¾	c	sugar
¼	c	quick-cooking tapioca
¼	tsp	ground cinnamon
¼	tsp	ground nutmeg
		Dash salt
2	c	fresh diced peaches
2	c	fresh diced pears
1	c	seedless green grapes
2	T	chopped maraschino cherries
1	T	lemon juice

In mixing bowl combin sugar, tapioca, cinnamon, nutmeg and dash salt. Add peaches, pears, grapes, maraschino cherries and lemon juice; toss. Let stand 5 minutes. Turn fruit mixture into the pastry-lined pie plate. Cut slits in top crust for escape of steam; place atop filling. Seal and flute edge. If desired, brush with milk; sprinkle with sugar. To prevent overbrowning, cover edge of pie with foil. Bake at 375° for 25 minutes. Remove foil; bake for 20 to 25 minutes longer or till golden. Cool pie on rack before serving.

EVERYDAY FRESH PEACH PIE

400° — 40-50 Minutes

5	c	fresh sliced peaches
¾	c	sugar
2	T	tapioca
1	T	lemon juice
1/8	tsp	cinnamon
		Few grains of salt
1	T	butter, cut into bits
		Pastry for two-crust 9-inch pie
1	tsp	sugar

Mix peaches, ¾ cup sugar, tapioca, lemon juice, cinnamon, salt and butter together. Line 9-inch pie pan with pastry. Pour peach mixture into crust; cover with top crust. Seal, flute, prick with fork. Brush lightly with cold water. Sprinkle with 1 teaspoon sugar. Bake at 400° for 40 to 50 minutes.

S.C. Department of Agriculture

FRESH PEACH UPSIDE DOWN PIE

450° — 10 Minutes
375° — 35-40 Minutes

		Pastry for two-crust 9-inch pie
2	T	soft butter
2/3	c	(4 oz) toasted sliced almonds or pecans
⅓	c	brown sugar
5	c	sliced fresh peaches
¾	c	sugar
¼	c	brown sugar
2	T	tapioca
½	tsp	nutmeg
¼	tsp	cinnamon

Line 9-inch pie pan with 12-inch square of foil. Let excess foil overhang edge. Spread with butter, press in nuts and ⅓ cup brown sugar. Fit bottom crust into pan over nuts and sugar. Mix rest of ingredients, pour into crust and cover with top crust. Seal, flute, prick with fork. Brush lightly with milk. Bake at 450° for 10 minutes, then at 375° for 35 to 40 minutes more. Cool thoroughly. Turn upside down on serving plate and remove foil.

National Peach Council

FRENCH CRUNCH PEACH PIE

400° — 25 Minutes

Serve with scoops of ice cream or cheese triangles.

1	can	(29 oz) sliced peaches
1		unbaked 9-inch pastry shell
1		egg, slightly beaten
1	T	lemon juice
⅓	c	sugar
1	c	vanilla wafer crumbs (about 24 cookies)
¼	c	butter or margarine, melted
½	c	toasted almonds, chopped

Drain peaches well and turn into pastry shell. Beat 1 egg slightly; stir in lemon juice and sugar. Pour over peaches. Mix crumbs, butter and almonds; sprinkle over filling. Bake at 400° about 25 minutes or till pastry is browned and filling is set in center. Cool thoroughly before cutting.

Makes 8 servings.

VERY EASIEST FRESH PEACH PIE 400° — 1 Hour

1		unbaked 9-inch pastry crust
1	c	sugar
3	T	flour
1/8	tsp	cinnamon
6		med-sized fresh peaches, quartered
2	T	butter

Mix sugar, flour and cinnamon. Sprinkle **half** of mixture over unbaked crust. Arrange peaches in single layer over mixture. Sprinkle with rest of sugar mixture. Dot with butter. Bake at 400° for about 1 hour, or until juices thicken and crust is light brown.

National Peach Council

SUMPTUOUS FRESH PEACH PIE 350° — 1 Hour, 10 Minutes

5	c	fresh sliced peaches
1		unbaked 9-inch pastry shell
⅓	c	butter or margarine, melted
1	c	sugar
⅓	c	all-purpose flour
1		egg

Place peaches in pastry shell. Combine remaining ingredients, and pour over peaches. Bake at 350° for 1 hour and 10 minutes.

CRUMB PEACH PIE 375° — 55 Minutes

1	c	unsifted flour
½	c	brown sugar, firmly packed
½	c	margarine
½	c	walnuts, chopped
3	T	cornstarch
½	tsp	ground ginger
½	c	light corn syrup
4½	c	peeled, sliced peaches
1		unbaked 9-inch pastry shell

In bowl stir together flour and sugar. With pastry blender or 2 knives cut in margarine until crumbs form. Stir in nuts; set aside. In medium bowl mix cornstarch and ginger. Stir in corn syrup until smooth. Add peaches. Toss to coat. Spoon into pastry shell. Sprinkle crumb mixture on top. Bake 375° for 55 minutes or until golden brown.

CARAMEL PEACH PIE 375° — 40-45 Minutes

1	can	peach pie filling
1		unbaked 9-inch pastry shell
1	pkg	caramel frosting mix (dry)
½	c	all-purpose flour
6	T	butter or margarine

Pour pie filling into pastry shell. Combine frosting mix and flour; cut in butter. Sprinkle over pie filling. Bake at 375° for 40 to 45 minutes.

It isn't the thing that we get, my friend,
And it isn't how much we know;
It's the will to serve, it's the hand we lend,
It's the light which our lanterns throw.

Charles R. Wakeley

GOLDEN PEACH PIE 375° — 20 Minutes + 25-30 Minutes

		Pastry for double-crust pie
3	cans	(16 oz ea) sliced peaches
½	c	sugar
2	T	all-purpose flour
½	tsp	ground nutmeg
		Dash salt
3	T	butter or margarine
½	tsp	finely shredded lemon peel
4	tsp	lemon juice
		Several drops almond extract
		Milk and sugar

Drain peaches, reserving ⅓ cup syrup; chop peach slices. In saucepan stir together sugar, flour, nutmeg and salt; add reserved syrup. Cook and stir till mixture is thickened and bubbly. Remove from heat. Stir in butter or margarine, lemon peel, lemon juice and almond extract; add drained chopped peaches. Turn mixture into pastry-lined pie plate. Cut slits in top crust; place pastry atop filling. Seal and flute edge. Brush with a little milk and sprinkle with some sugar. To prevent overbrowning, cover edge of pie with foil. Bake at 375° for 20 minutes. Remove foil and bake 25 to 30 minutes more or till crust is golden. Serve pie warm.

FRESH PEACH PIE FILLING

4	qts	sliced peaches
2	tsp	ascorbic acid
3½	c	sugar
1	tsp	salt
½	c	plus 2 T minute tapioca
⅓	c	lemon juice

Peel and slice 4 quarts peaches into ascorbic acid water. Combine 2 teaspoons ascorbic acid, sugar, salt and tapioca; mix with drained peaches. Add lemon juice and mix well. Freeze filling in pie shapes* or in four one-quart freezer containers.

Yield: 4 quarts.

*To freeze pie shapes: Line four 8-inch pie pans with aluminum foil, freezer paper or film, letting the lining extend five inches beyond rim of pans. Measure four cups filling in each pan. Loosely cover filling with lining. Freeze until firm. Seal lining tightly over filling. Remove from pans, wrap air-tight in freezer paper and return to freezer. To bake pies: line a 9-inch pie pan with pastry and trim pastry. Sprinkle bottom crust with one tablespoon flour. Remove wrapping from pie-shaped frozen filling and set the frozen block of fruit into the pastry-lined pan. Do not thaw. Dot filling with one tablespoon butter. Moisten edge of bottom crust. Cover with top crust and flute edges. Be sure slits are open in upper crust to permit steam to escape while baking. Bake at 425° for 10 minutes. Reduce temperature to 350° for about 1 hour or until syrup boils with heavy bubbles.

Georgia Peach Commission

CINNAMON FRUIT CRISP   350° — 30-35 Minutes

½	c	quick-cooking rolled oats
½	c	packed brown sugar
¼	c	all-purpose flour
½	tsp	ground cinnamon
		Dash salt
¼	c	butter or margarine
5	c	peeled and sliced peaches
2	T	granulated sugar

In medium bowl combine oats, brown sugar, flour, cinnamon and salt. Cut in butter or margarine till mixture resembles coarse crumbs; set aside. Place peaches in 10x6x2-inch baking dish. Sprinkle with granulated sugar. Sprinkle oat mixture over peaches. Bake at 350° for 30 to 35 minutes or till fruit is tender.

Makes 6 servings.

FRESH PEACH PIE   400° — 40-50 Minutes

3	c	peeled, sliced peaches
1	c	sugar
3	T	all-purpose flour
		Pastry for two-crust pie
1	T	brown sugar
2	T	butter or margarine
		Cinnamon sugar

Mix peaches, sugar and flour together; set aside. Line a 9- inch pie plate with one pastry. Sprinkle brown sugar and dot with butter. Add peach mixture; cover with top pastry. Fold top pastry edge over bottom edge and pinch to seal. Place a few slits in the top crust to allow steam to escape. Brush top crust with milk and sprinkle it with cinnamon sugar. Bake at 400° for 40 to 50 minutes or until crust is golden brown.

Tip: A strip of foil placed around the crust edge for the first 30 minutes will prevent over-browning.

Georgia Peach Commission

BUTTERSCOTCH PEACH PIE   450° — 15 Minutes
                                     350° — 35 Minutes

		Pastry for 2-crust, 9-inch pie
4	c	fresh peeled and sliced peaches
¼	c	brown sugar, firmly packed
2	T	flour
2	tsp	lemon juice
6	T	melted butter
½	tsp	nutmeg
¼	tsp	almond extract

Fit one pastry in bottom of a 9-inch pie plate. Arrange peaches in pie shell. In small bowl, combine remaining ingredients. Sprinkle over peaches. Top with remaining crust, crimp edges and slash top for steam to escape. Bake at 450° for 15 minutes; reduce heat to 350° and bake 35 to 40 minutes more, or until golden. Serve warm or cold.

California Tree Fruit Agreement

CRISPY PEACH DESSERT   350° — 25-35 Minutes

6		to 8 peaches, peeled and halved
¼	c	brown sugar
½	c	sifted flour
1/8	tsp	nutmeg
¼	c	margarine

Place peaches in buttered dish. Combine other ingredients and mix together to consistency of fine crumbs. Sprinkle over peaches. Bake at 350° for 25 to 30 minutes. Serve warm.

NO-BAKE FRESH PEACH CRISP

1	c	sugar
3	T	cornstarch
		Pinch of salt
½	c	water
1/8	tsp	almond flavoring, optional
3-4	c	fresh sliced peaches
2	c	"natural" cereal

OR
"Make Your Own Topping"*

Into a medium size saucepan measure ¼ **cup** sugar. Add cornstarch, salt and water. Stir to dissolve, then cook over medium heat stirring constantly until mixture thickens. Add the remaining ¾ **cup** sugar and return to heat and cook until sugar is dissolved. Add almond flavoring and fresh peaches. Stir to mix thoroughly. Pour into an 8-inch square pan or pie pan. Top with cereal mixture OR the fresh peach mixture can be poured directly into individual serving dishes and then topped with cereal mixture. Serve with cream, whipped topping or ice cream.

*Make Your Own Topping: Mix ½ cup flour, 5 tablespoons brown sugar, ½ cup quick cooking oats and 1 tablespoon sesame seeds (optional). Add 5 tablespoons butter and cut into flour mixture as for pastry. Pour onto a cookie sheet and spread mixture evenly. Bake at 300° for 20 minutes, stirring frequently until mixture is brown. Let cool thoroughly. Store in an air-tight container in a cool place. Will keep up to a month when stored properly.

S.C. Department of Agriculture

PEACH BROWN BETTY   350°

1	can	(20 oz) sliced peaches
3	c	dry bread crumbs
½	c	melted butter
1	c	light brown sugar, packed
½	tsp	salt
½	tsp	cinnamon
		Juice of ½ lemon

Place the peaches and bread crumbs in a bowl. Add the butter, sugar, salt, cinnamon and lemon juice and mix well. Pour into a greased casserole. Bake at 350° until lightly browned. Serve with lemon sauce, whipped cream or ice cream.

BONANZA OF PEACH DUMPLINGS
425° — 40 Minutes

2-2½ c		all-purpose flour
2	tsp	baking powder
1	tsp	salt
¾	c	shortening
½	c	whole milk
4	md	peaches, peeled and halved
1	c	sugar
1¼	tsp	ground cinnamon
1½	c	water
2	T	butter or margarine
		Dash of ground nutmeg
		Whipping cream

Combine flour, baking powder and salt; cut in shortening with pastry blender until mixture resembles coarse meal. Gradually add milk, stirring to make a soft dough. Roll dough into a 14-inch square (¼-inch thickness) on a lightly floured surface; then cut dough into four 7-inch squares. Place 2 peach halves on each square. Sprinkle each (2 halves) with **2 teaspoons** sugar and **1/8 teaspoon** cinnamon. Moisten edges of each dumpling with water; bring corners to center, pinching edges to seal. Place dumplings 1 inch apart in a lightly greased shallow baking pan. Combine water, butter, **¼ teaspoon** cinnamon and dash of nutmeg in a medium saucepan; place over low heat, stirring until butter melts and sugar dissolves. Pour syrup over dumplings. Bake at 425° for 40-45 minutes or until golden brown. Serve with cream.
Makes 4 servings.

OVEN PEACHY-PLUM TURNOVERS

375⁰ — 15 Minutes

¾	c	sugar
½	tsp	ginger
1	c	fresh diced peaches
2		pkgs (3 oz each) cream cheese, softened
4½	c	buttermilk baking mix
1	c	water
4	c	fresh plums, thickly sliced
1		egg, lightly beaten
		Granulated Sugar

In small bowl, combine sugar and ginger; set aside. In mixing bowl, stir peaches into cream cheese; set aside. In another bowl, measure baking mix. Make well in center, add water. Stir with fork to make soft dough. On floured board, knead 3 or 4 times to smooth. Divide dough into 12 equal balls; roll each into a 6 inch circle. Arrange ⅓ cup of plum wedges on half of each circle, leaving ½ inch margin around edge. Sprinkle 1 tablespoon sugar mixture over plums on each circle; top with generous tablespoon of cheese mixture. For each turnover, moisten edges with water; fold dough over filling to form a half circle. Press edges together with tines of fork to seal completely. Place turnovers on baking sheets. Brush with egg; sprinkle generously with sugar. Bake at 375⁰ for 15 to 20 minutes or until golden. Cool on rack 5 minutes. Serve warm or cold. Turnovers can be made ahead and reheated.

Yield: 12 turnovers. *California Tree Fruit Agreement*

LUCIOUS PEACH DUMPLINGS

400⁰ — 45 Minutes

1	can	(29 oz) sliced peaches
2	c	sugar
		Cinnamon to taste
2	c	flour
½	tsp	salt
2	tsp	baking powder
½	c	shortening
¾	c	water, about
1		stick butter or margarine

Mix the peaches, sugar and cinnamon and set aside. Sift the flour, salt and baking powder together into a bowl and cut in shortening. Add enough water to make a soft dough. Roll out on floured board to a rectangle and cut into squares. Fill pastry squares with sweetened peaches and dot with butter. Fold pastry over and seal edges. Place in a baking dish. Bake at 400⁰ for about 45 minutes. Serve with whipped cream, if desired.

FRESH PEACH DUMPLINGS

425° — 10 Minutes
350° — 30 Minutes

1	c	dark corn syrup
½	c	water
¼	c	lemon juice
1	tsp	grated lemon peel
2	T	butter or margarine
2	c	all-purpose flour
2	tsp	baking powder
½	tsp	salt
½	c	shortening
¾	c	whole milk
2½	c	sliced peaches
½	c	sugar
¼	tsp	EACH cinnamon and nutmeg

Combine corn syrup, water, lemon juice and lemon peel in a saucepan. Bring to a boil and simmer 10 minutes. Add butter and remove syrup mixture from heat. Mix flour, baking powder and salt together. Cut in shortening. Add milk and stir just until moistened. Roll out ½-inch thick and cut into eight 5-inch squares. Combine peaches, sugar, cinnamon and nutmeg. Place 2 tablespoons of the peach mixture on each square. Fold corners to center and pinch edges to seal. Arrange pouches in a greased 8x12-inch baking dish. Pour syrup mixture over dumplings, moistening each. Bake at 425° for 10 minutes. Reduce heat to 350° and bake 30 minutes longer. Serve warm.

Makes 8 servings.

Georgia Peach Commission

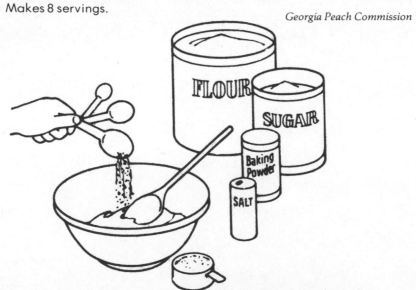

FANCY FRUIT TART

Citrus Glaze

1	T	cornstarch
¼	c	water
¾	c	orange juice
1	T	lemon juice
¼	tsp	grated lemon rind

Combine cornstarch, water and orange juice in a small saucepan. Bring to a boil; cook over medium heat 1 minute, stirring constantly. Remove from heat; stir in lemon juice and grated lemon rind. Cover surface with waxed paper or plastic wrap; let cool.

Yield: about 1 cup glaze.

Tart   400° — 8-10 Minutes

1	c	all-purpose flour
¼	c	cornstarch
¼	c	sugar
2/3	c	margarine
1		egg, beaten
		Vegetable cooking spray
1	c	fresh sliced peaches
1	c	fresh sliced strawberries
½	c	seedless green grapes, halved
¼	c	fresh blueberries

Combine flour, cornstarch and sugar; cut in margarine with pastry blender until mixture resembles coarse meal. Add egg, and stir with a fork until all ingredients are moistened. Spray a 14x12-inch baking sheet with cooking spray. Shape dough into a ball, and place directly on baking sheet. Roll pastry into a circle (the size of a serving platter); trim edge. Bake at 400° for 8 to 10 minutes; then carefully remove to wire rack to complete cooling. Place pastry on a serving platter, and arrange fruit attractively over top; spoon Citrus Glaze evenly over fruit. Refrigerate tart at least 1 hour before serving.

Makes 10 servings.

STUFFED PEACH PIE   425° — 20 Minutes

Pastry for one-crust pie
1	c	crushed macaroons
6		fresh peaches
½	c	brown sugar, firmly packed
¼	c	chopped walnuts
2	T	maple syrup

Prepare favorite pie pastry and set aside. Crush macaroons and place in bottom of an 8-inch pie plate. Peel, halve and remove pits from peaches. In a small bowl, combine brown sugar, walnuts and syrup, mixing thoroughly. Place a heaping teaspoon of the brown sugar mixture in six peach halves. Gently press other halves on top of stuffed halves. Arrange in pie plate. Roll out pastry and place on top of peaches, sealing edges. Bake at 425° for 20 minutes until pastry is lightly browned. Serve with New England Nutmeg Sauce.*

Makes 6 servings.

*New England Nutmeg Sauce
1	c	sugar
1	T	flour
1	c	boiling water
1	T	butter
1	tsp	nutmeg
1	T	fresh lemon juice

Combine sugar and flour together in a saucepan. Add boiling water and cook, stirring constantly until sauce thickens slightly. Add butter and simmer gently for 5 minutes. Remove from heat and stir in nutmeg and lemon juice. Serve warm.   *California Tree Fruit Agreement*

FRESH PEACH COOKIE COBBLER   350° — 55 Minutes

4	c	fresh sliced peaches
1	c	sugar
3	T	tapioca
		Dash of nutmeg
2	tsp	ascorbic acid powder
1		roll refrigerator cookie dough

Thoroughly mix peaches, sugar, tapioca, nutmeg and ascorbic acid powder. Set aside. Slice cookie dough as for baking in ½-inch thick slices. Line bottom and sides of 9-inch square baking dish with slices of cookie dough. Pour peach mixture over the slices and top with remaining slices. Bake at 350° for approximately 55 minutes, or until cookie dough is brown and done.

Makes 6 servings.

National Peach Council

PEACH CRISP   325° — 30 Minutes

6		or 7 peaches, peeled and sliced
		Juice of 1 lemon
½	c	sifted all-purpose flour
¾	c	rolled oats
½	c	brown sugar, packed
⅓	c	margarine

Put peaches in shallow 2-quart baking dish and sprinkle with lemon juice. Mix flour, oats and brown sugar. Cut in margarine with pastry blender. Press over peaches. Bake at 325° for 30 minutes or until peaches are tender. Serve warm with Hard Sauce.*

Makes 6 servings.

*Hard Sauce

¼	c	butter
¾	c	powdered sugar
½	tsp	vanilla
1	T	hot water

Rub butter with the back of a spoon until very creamy; stir in sugar very gradually; stir in vanilla gradually. Stir in hot water a few drops at a time to prevent separation of the sauce. Pile lightly in a serving dish; chill thoroughly.

Georgia Peach Commission

DEEP DISH FRESH PEACH PIE   350° — 1 Hour

5	c	sliced fresh peaches
2	T	flour
¾	c	sugar
½	tsp	cinnamon
1	tsp	butter
1	pkg	ready-to-bake refrigerated cookie dough

Mix peaches, flour, sugar and cinnamon. Put into 8-inch square baking pan. Cut butter into small pieces over top of peaches. Arrange ½-inch slices of cookie dough in rows over top of peaches. Bake at 350° for 1 hour. Cool about 2 hours before serving. Top with whipped cream or ice cream.

Makes 6 to 8 servings.

National Peach Council

FAVORITE PEACH KUCHEN
400° — 15 Minutes + 30 Minutes

2	c	sifted flour
¼	tsp	baking powder
½	tsp	salt
7/8	c	sugar
		Sliced fresh peaches
1	tsp	cinnamon
2		egg yolks, beaten
1	c	sour cream

Combine the flour, baking powder, salt and **2 tablespoons** sugar in a bowl. Cut in the butter until mixture is consistency of cornmeal. Press into 8-inch square pan. Cover with peaches and sprinkle with remaining sugar and cinnamon. Bake at 400° for 15 minutes. Mix the egg yolks and sour cream and pour over peaches. Bake for 30 minutes longer and serve hot or cold.

TASTY PEACH KUCHEN
350° — 15 Minutes + 15 Minutes

1½	c	all-purpose flour
¼	c	sugar
1	T	baking powder
¼	tsp	salt
2		eggs, slightly beaten
½	c	whole milk
½	c	shortening, melted
1		carton (8 oz) dairy sour cream
⅓	c	sugar
3		peaches, peeled, pitted and sliced
		Ground cinnamon

In mixing bowl stir together flour, **¼ cup** sugar, baking powder and salt. Combine **1 egg**, milk and melted shortening; add to flour mixture. Mix well. Spread in a greased 9x9x2-inch baking pan. Bake at 350° for 15 minutes. Remove from oven. In bowl combine **1 egg**, sour cream and **⅓ cup** sugar. Spread evenly over partially baked crust. Arrange peach slices atop. Sprinkle cinnamon over peaches. Continue baking 15 minutes more. Do not overbake. Cool on wire rack. Serve warm or chilled.
Makes 10 servings.

SO GOOD PEACH PASTRIES

Baked individual pastry shells

⅓	c	plus 2 T sugar
2	T	cornstarch
		Dash salt
1	c	whole milk
1	pkg	(3 oz) cream cheese, softened
2	T	milk
1		egg yolk, slightly beaten
½	tsp	vanilla
1		egg white
		Sliced peaches

In saucepan combine ⅓ **cup** sugar, cornstarch and salt. Gradually stir in 1 cup milk. Cook and stir till thickened and bubbly. Remove from heat. In small bowl combine cream cheese, 2 tablespoons milk and the slightly beaten egg yolk. Gradually stir cream cheese mixture into the hot mixture, stirring constantly. Return mixture to heat; bring to gentle boil. Cook and stir 2 minutes more. Remove from heat; stir in vanilla. Beat egg white till soft peaks form. Gradually add the **2 tablespoons** sugar, beating to stiff peaks; fold into pudding. Spoon filling into baked tart shells. Cover; chill before serving. At serving time top with peach slices and garnish with fresh mint or chopped nuts.

FRESH PEACH PICNIC PIES

450° — 15 Minutes
350° — 30 Minutes

1	pkg	(11 oz) pie crust mix
	OR	pastry for 2-crust pie
4		fresh peaches, peeled and quartered
½	c	sugar
2	T	cornstarch
		Dash salt
		Dash nutmeg
1	T	lemon juice
4		aluminum foil tart pans (5 inches in diameter)

Prepare pastry, as package directs. Divide into 4 parts. On lightly floured board, roll each part into a 7-inch circle. Ease pastry circles into tart pans. Place 4 peach quarters in pastry-lined pans. In small bowl, combine sugar, cornstarch, salt and nutmeg. Sprinkle mixture and lemon juice onto peaches, dividing equally. Gather edges of pastry up around peaches, pinching slightly. Brush pastry with milk or beaten egg and sprinkle with sugar, if desired. Bake at 450° for 15 minutes; then reduce heat to 350° and continue baking 30 minutes more. Serve warm or cold.

Makes 4 servings.

California Tree Fruit Agreement

MY FAVORITE PEACH COBBLER   375° — 30-35 Minutes

4	c	sliced peaches
1	tsp	lemon juice
1	c	sugar
1	c	SELF-RISING flour
1		egg
1		stick margarine

Slice peaches into casserole dish; add lemon juice. Mix sugar, flour and egg and crumble over top of peaches. Pour margarine over top and bake at 375° for 30-35 minutes.

PEACH QUEEN'S FAVORITE   375° — 40 Minutes

Excellent served warm.

1		stick margarine
1	c	whole milk
1	c	SELF-RISING flour
1	c	sugar
4	c	sliced peaches, sweetened to taste

Melt margarine in a 9x12-inch baking dish. Combine milk, flour and sugar and mix thoroughly; add to the melted margarine. Add peaches and do not stir. Bake at 375° for approximately 40 minutes or until browned. Top with whipped cream or vanilla ice cream, if desired. (Canned or frozen peaches may be substituted for fresh.)
Makes 8 servings.

S.C. Department of Agriculture

OLD FASHIONED PEACH COBBLER   350° — 45 Minutes

2	c	fresh peaches
1¾	c	sugar
1		stick margarine
1	c	all-purpose flour
1	tsp	baking powder
1	c	whole milk

Combine peaches and ¾ **cup** sugar; let stand 20 minutes. Melt margarine in 1½-quart baking dish in oven. Sift together flour, **1 cup** sugar, and baking powder. Add milk and stir briskly - lumps will remain. Pour into baking dish of melted butter; top with peaches. Bake at 350° for 45 minutes.

S.C. Department of Agriculture

SPECTACULAR PEACH COBBLER 350° — 35 Minutes
+ 40 Minutes

4	c	fresh sliced peaches
1	c	sugar
½	c	butter or margarine
1½	c	all-purpose flour
¾	tsp	salt
½	c	shortening
¼	c	plus 1 T cold water

Combine peaches, sugar and butter in a medium saucepan; bring to a boil and cook over low heat until peaches are tender and mixture thickens. Pour peach mixture into a lightly buttered 10x6x2-inch baking dish. Set aside. Combine flour and salt; cut in shortening with a pastry blender until mixture resembles coarse meal. Sprinkle water evenly over flour mixture and stir with a fork until all ingredients are moistened. Shape pastry into a ball. Roll out pastry to 1/8-inch thickness on a lightly floured board; cut into 1-inch strips and arrange half of the strips in lattice design over peaches. Bake at 350° for 35 minutes. Remove from oven, and gently press baked pastry into peach mixture. Repeat lattice design over peaches with remaining pastry strips. Return to oven and bake an additional 40 minutes.

BLUEBERRY PEACH COBBLER 350° — 50 Minutes

1	c	sugar
1	c	all-purpose flour
2	tsp	baking powder
1	tsp	salt
1	c	whole milk
½	c	butter or margarine, melted
3	med	peaches, peeled, sliced and lightly sugared
2/3	c	fresh or frozen blueberries
		Vanilla ice cream, optional

Combine dry ingredients in a medium mixing bowl. Combine milk and butter; pour over dry ingredients, and mix until smooth. Pour into a greased 12x8x2-inch glass baking dish. Spread peaches evenly over top of batter; sprinkle with blueberries. Bake at 350° for 50 minutes or until batter rises through the fruit and top is golden brown. Serve cobbler warm and topped with vanilla ice cream, if desired.
Makes 8 to 10 servings.

IRRESISTABLE FRUIT COBBLER

Peach Filling

½	c	brown sugar, packed
4	tsp	cornstarch
¼	tsp	ground nutmeg
½	c	water
4	c	fresh peeled and sliced peaches
1	T	lemon juice
1	T	butter

Combine brown sugar, cornstarch and ground nutmeg. Stir in water; cook and stir till thickened and bubbly. Stir in peaches, lemon juice and butter; heat through. Keep warm.

Topping

1	c	all-purpose flour
2	T	sugar
1½	tsp	baking powder
¼	tsp	salt
¼	c	butter or margarine
1		egg, slightly beaten
¼	c	whole milk

Stir together flour, sugar, baking powder and salt. Cut in butter till mixture resembles coarse crumbs. Combine egg and milk; add all at once to flour mixture. Stir just to moisten. Turn hot filling into a 1½-quart casserole. Immediately spoon "topping" in 6 mounds on top of peach mixture in casserole. Bake at 400° for 20 minutes.

Makes 6 servings.

EASY PEACH COBBLER   375° — 30 Minutes

¼	c	margarine
½	c	sugar
1		egg
½	c	whole milk
1	c	all-purpose flour
1	tsp	baking powder
1	qt	peeled, sliced peaches, lightly sugared
2	T	lemon juice

Cream margarine and sugar. Add egg and beat well; add milk. Sift flour and baking powder together and add. Combine peaches and lemon juice and place in baking dish. Spoon the batter over the peaches and bake at 375° until the crust is brown, about 30 minutes.

PEACH BREAD   350⁰ — 45-55 Minutes

2	c	all-purpose flour
½	c	sugar
½	c	brown sugar, firmly packed
1/8	tsp	salt
1	tsp	baking soda
2	c	very ripe mashed peaches
1	lg	egg, slightly beaten
2	T	butter or margarine, melted
½	c	raisins OR nuts

In a bowl, mix together flour, sugars, salt and baking soda. Drain mashed peaches and put in large bowl. Add beaten egg, melted butter or margarine. Stir in raisins **or** nuts. Stir in flour mixture. Pour into 9x5-inch greased and floured loaf pan. Let stand 20 minutes. Bake at 350⁰ for 45 to 55 minutes. Cool bread in pan 15 minutes; remove from pan and finish cooling on wire rack. (Peach Bread freezes beautifully for later use). Yield: 1 loaf bread.

Note: This is a moist, tender bread. It will cut more evenly and neatly, therefore, if made the day before serving.

National Peach Council

BROWN-SUGARED PEACH MUFFINS   400° — 20-25 Minutes

4	c	all-purpose flour
2/3	c	brown sugar, pakced
2	T	baking powder
1	tsp	salt
½	tsp	baking soda
¼	tsp	ground allspice
2		eggs
2	c	dairy sour cream
½	c	cooking oil
1	c	fresh, frozen, or canned peaches, chopped

In large mixing bowl stir together the flour, sugar, baking powder, salt, baking soda and allspice. Make a well in the center. Combine the eggs, sour cream and oil; stir in peaches. Add peach mixture all at once to the flour mixture. Stir just till moistened; batter should be lumpy. Spoon batter into greased or paper-lined muffin cups, filling each about 2/3 full. Bake at 400° for 20 to 25 minutes or till golden. Remove from pans, serve warm.

Yield: about 20 muffins.

BRAN-PEACH MUFFINS   400° — 20-25 Minutes

1½	c	whole bran cereal
1	c	whole milk
1		egg, beaten
¼	c	cooking oil
1	c	all-purpose flour
¼ - ⅓	c	sugar
2	tsp	baking powder
½	tsp	baking soda
½	tsp	ground cinnamon
½	tsp	lemon peel, finely shredded
½	tsp	salt
1	c	fresh peeled and sliced peaches

In medium bowl combine bran and milk; let stand 3 minutes or till liquid is absorbed. Stir in egg and oil. In another medium bowl stir together flour, sugar, baking powder, soda, cinnamon, lemon peel and salt. Add bran mixture all at once to flour mixture, stirring just till moistened; batter will be thick. Fold in peaches. Fill greased or paper-lined muffin cups 2/3 full. Bake at 400° for 20 to 25 minutes.

Yield: 15 muffins.

LUSCIOUS PEACH CRESCENTS   375° — 20 Minutes

1	can	(8 oz) refrigerated crescent dinner rolls
		About 3 T commercial sour cream
		About 6 T peach marmalade
¼	c	chopped walnuts
¼	c	flaked coconut
2	T	peach marmalade, melted
		Additional chopped walnuts, optional

Separate crescent rolls into triangles. Spread each triangle with about 1 teaspoon sour cream and about 2 teaspoons marmalade. Sprinkle each evenly with walnuts and coconut; roll up, beginning at large end. Place seam side down, 1 inch apart on a greased baking sheet; curve into a crescent. Bake at 375° for 20 minutes or until golden brown. Remove from oven, and brush with melted margarine; sprinkle with additional walnuts, if desired.

Makes 6 to 8 servings.

IRRESISTABLE PEACH SWIRLS   450° — 20 Minutes

1	can	refrigerated crescent rolls
2	T	butter or margarine, melted
1	c	finely chopped peaches
1	tsp	ascorbic acid powder
¼	tsp	sugar

Remove rolls from can. Do not separate. Place on lightly floured board and work them into a rectangle about ¼-inch thick. Brush with melted butter. Mix chopped peaches with ascorbic acid powder and sugar. Sprinkle over surface of dough. Sprinkle with nutmeg. Roll up jellyroll fashion beginning with the long side of the dough. Cut into nine equal slices. Place swirls in buttered dish, cut side down. Dot with butter, if desired. Bake at 450° for 20 minutes. Ice with peach glaze; mix 1 cup sifted powdered sugar with 1 ½ tablespoons fresh peach puree until smooth and drizzle over baked swirls. Top with chopped pecans if desired.

Yield: 9 swirls.

Georgia Peach Commission

For a gift with a special touch, peach bread can be baked in a 6x3x2-inch tinfoil loaf pan for gift-giving.

GEORGIA PEACH BREAD   325°—55 Minutes

1½	c	sugar
½	c	shortening
2		eggs
2¼	c	pureed peaches
2	c	all-purpose flour
1	tsp	EACH cinnamon, soda, baking powder
¼	tsp	salt
1	tsp	vanilla
1	c	finely chopped pecans

Cream sugar and shortening together. Add eggs and mix thoroughly. Add peach puree and dry ingredients. Mix thoroughly. Add vanilla and chopped pecans and stir until blended. Pour into two loaf pans (approx. 5x9) that have been well greased and floured. Bake at 325° for 55 minutes to 1 hour. Let bread cool a few minutes before removing from pan.

Yield: 2 loaves bread.

Georgia Peach Commission

DELECTABLE PEACH JAM BREAD   350° — 40-45 Minutes

1½	c	all-purpose flour
¾	tsp	salt
½	tsp	baking soda
½	tsp	ground cinnamon
½	tsp	ground nutmeg
¾	c	sugar
⅓	c	shortening
2		eggs
¾	c	peach jam
½	tsp	vanilla
½	c	buttermilk

In mixing bowl stir together flour, salt, soda, cinnamon and nutmeg; set aside. In large mixing bowl beat the sugar and shortening on high speed of electric mixer till light and fluffy. Beat in the eggs, one at a time, beating 1 minute after each. Add peach jam and vanilla; mix well. Add flour mixture and buttermilk alternately to creamed mixture, beating well after each addition. Pour batter into two greased and floured 6x3x2-inch loaf pans. Bake at 350° for 40 to 45 minutes or till wooden pick inserted near center comes out clean. Cool in pans 10 minutes. Remove from pans. Cool thoroughly on wire racks.

Yield: 2 loaves.

PEACH PECAN BREAD   375⁰ — 60-65 Minutes

2	c	unsifted all-purpose flour
2	tsp	baking powder
½	tsp	ground nutmeg
½	tsp	salt
½	c	corn oil margarine
¾	c	light corn syrup
¼	c	sugar
2		eggs
1	c	EACH peeled, mashed peaches and chopped pecans

Grease 9x5x3-inch loaf pan. In small bowl stir together flour, baking powder, nutmeg and salt. In large bowl with mixer at medium speed beat margarine until softened. Add corn syrup and sugar; beat until smooth. Add eggs; beat 1 to 2 minutes or until light. (Mixture will look curdled.) Stir in flour mixture alternately with peaches. Stir in pecans. Turn into prepared pan. Bake at 375⁰ for 60 to 65 minutes or until cake tester inserted in center comes out clean. Cool 10 minutes in pan. Remove from pan. Cool completely on wire rack. Wrap in foil or plastic wrap. Bread slices best when stored overnight.

Yield: 1 loaf bread   *Georgia Peach Commission*

DELICIOUS PEACH BREAD   350⁰ — 1 Hour

½	c	butter or margarine, softened
1	c	sugar
3		eggs
2¾	c	all-purpose flour
1½	tsp	baking powder
1	tsp	salt
½	tsp	baking soda
1½	tsp	ground cinnamon
2	c	fresh sliced peaches
3	T	frozen orange juice concentrate, thawed and undiluted
t	tsp	vanilla extract

Cream butter; gradually add sugar, beating well. Add eggs, one at a time, beating well after each addition. Combine flour, baking powder, salt, soda and cinnamon; add to creamed mixture alternately with the peaches, beginning and ending with flour mixture. Stir in orange juice concentrate and vanilla. Pour batter into a greased and floured 9x5x3-inch loaf pan. Bake at 350⁰ for 1 hour or until wooden pick inserted in center comes out clean. Cool in pan 10 minutes; remove from pan, and cool completely.

Yield: 1 loaf bread.

PEACHY PECAN BREAD   350° — 1 Hour

Remember, bread seems to slice better after being refrigerated.

2	c	peaches, home canned
	OR	
1	can	(16 oz) sliced peaches
6	T	butter, melted
2		eggs
1	T	lemon juice
2	c	all-purpose flour
¾	c	sugar
3	tsp	baking powder
1	tsp	salt
¾	c	chopped pecans
2	T	peach preserves

Drain peaches, reserving ¼ cup syrup. Finely chop **1 cup** peaches and set aside. In blender combine remaining peaches, butter, eggs, reserved peach syrup and lemon juice. Blend until just smooth. Stir together dry ingredients. Add egg mixture and stir until moistened. Fold in reserved peaches and nuts. Bake in greased 8x4x2-inch loaf pan at 350° for 1 hour. Spread with peach preserves. Cool in pan 10 minutes, remove and cool on rack.

Yield: 1 loaf.   *S.C. Department of Agriculture*

PIZZA PEACH PIE   350° — 15-20 Minutes

½	c	butter or margarine
¼	c	sifted confectioners' sugar
1	c	sifted all-purpose flour
2	T	cornstarch
2	T	granulated sugar
¼	tsp	mace
2/3	c	orange juice
½	c	red currant jelly
1	can	(29 oz) sliced peaches, well drained

Crust: Cream together butter or margarine and confectioners' sugar. Blend in flour to make soft dough. Pat evenly onto bottom and sides of 12-inch pizza pan; prick well with fork. Bake in moderate oven 350° for 15 to 20 minutes. Let cool.

Glaze: Combine cornstarch, granulated sugar, and mace in small saucepan. Stir in orange juice; add jelly. Cook and stir till mixture thickens and boils; cook 2 minutes more. Cool slightly. Arrange peaches in single layer in baked shell, forming circles, one inside the other. Spoon glaze over. Chill. Top with whipped cream.

Makes 10 to 12 servings.

FRESH PEACH PIZZA
375° — 35-40 Minutes

Pastry:

1⅔	c	all-purpose flour
1½	tsp	baking powder
		Pinch of salt
		Dash of nutmeg
4	T	butter or margarine
1		egg
¼	c	whole milk

Mix dry ingredients together, add butter and cut in until crumbly. Add milk to beaten eggs, mix well and add to flour mixture. Stir to form a soft dough. Place dough in a greased 13-inch pizza pan. Press over bottom of pan with waxed paper.

Filling:

3	c	sliced peaches
1	pkg	(3 oz) peach flavored gelatin
¼	tsp	almond flavoring

Mix peaches, gelatin and flavoring until gelatin is moist. Pour over dough, carefully spreading sliced peaches to the edge of pastry.

TOPPING:

⅓	c	granulated sugar
⅓	c	brown sugar, firmly packed
⅓	c	all-purpose flour
⅓	c	oatmeal
4	T	butter or margarine
⅓	c	almond slivers

Mix sugars, flour and oatmeal; cut in butter or margarine. Add almond slivers. Sprinkle over peaches. Bake at 375° for 35 to 40 minutes.
Makes 8 to 10 servings.

Georgia Peach Commission

So, friend, my wish is that we may
See Good in all who pass our way.

Phil Perkins

*Find your favorite among the four variations of the famous
Thumbprint Cookie!*

THUMBPRINT COOKIES #1

325°—20 Minutes

1	c	margarine, softened
½	c	sugar
½	c	dark corn syrup
2		eggs, separated
2½	c	unsifted flour
2	c	walnuts, finely chopped
		Peach Jam or Marmalade

In large bowl with mixer at medium speed beat margarine and sugar until smooth. Beat in corn syrup and egg yolks until well mixed. Stir in flour until well blended. Chill dough 20 to 25 minutes or until firm enough to handle. Shape into 1-inch balls. Dip into slightly beaten egg white. Roll in nuts. Place 2 inches apart on greased cookie sheet. With thumb make indentation in center of each cookie. Bake at 325° for 20 minutes or until golden. Remove from oven. While still warm fill with a small amount of jam. Cool on wire rack.

Yield: about 4 dozen.

THUMBPRINT COOKIES #2   375°F—5 Min + 8 Min

¼	c	shortening
¼	c	butter or margarine
¼	c	brown sugar, firmly packed
1		egg, separated
½	tsp	vanilla extract
1	c	all-purpose flour
¼	tsp	salt
¾	c	nuts, finely chopped
		Peach Jam or Preserves

Cream shortening and butter with sugar; add egg **yolk** and vanilla extract. Add flour and salt; blend well. Roll dough into 1-inch balls; dip in slightly beatened egg white. Roll in nuts and place 1 inch apart on ungreased cookie sheet. Bake at 375° for 5 minutes, remove from oven and quickly press thumb in center of each cookie, return to oven and bake 8 minutes longer. Cool. Place jam or preserves in thumbprint.

Yield: 2 dozen cookies.

THUMBPRINT COOKIES #3   350° — 15-17 Minutes

2/3	c	butter or margarine
1/3	c	granulated sugar
2		eggs, separated
1	tsp	vanilla
1/2	tsp	salt
1½	c	sifted all-purpose flour
3/4	c	finely chopped walnuts
		Peach jam or preserves

Cream together butter or margarine and sugar until fluffy. Add egg **yolks** (reserve egg whites), 1 teaspoon vanilla and salt; beat well. Gradually add flour, mixing well. Shape dough in ¾-inch balls; dip in egg whites, slightly beaten, then roll in chopped walnuts. Place 1 inch apart on greased cookie sheet. Press down center of each with thumb. Bake cookies at 350° oven for 15 to 17 minutes or till done. Cool slightly; remove from sheet and cool on rack. Just before serving, fill centers with peach jam or preserves.

Yield: about 3 dozen cookies.

THUMBPRINT COOKIES #4   350° — 10-12 Minutes

1½	c	butter or margarine
1¼	c	sugar
1		egg
3/4	c	peanut butter
3½	c	all-purpose flour
		Peach jam or preserves

In mixer bowl beat butter or margarine on medium speed of electric mixer for 30 seconds. Add the sugar; beat till creamy. Add egg and peanut butter; beat well. Add flour; beat till well blended. Cover and chill about 1 hour. Using 1 tablespoon dough for each, shape into 1¼-inch balls; place on ungreased cookie sheets. Press down centers with thumb. Fill centers with peach jam. Bake at 350° for 10 to 12 minutes or till done. Remove to wire rack to cool.

Yield: about 7 dozen cookies.

There are two worlds: the world that we can measure with line and rule, and the world that we feel with our hearts and imagination.

Leigh Hunt

PEACH COOKIES   375⁰ — 20 Minutes

½	c	margarine or butter
1	c	sugar
1	lg	egg
2	c	all-purpose flour
½	tsp	baking soda
¼	tsp	EACH nutmeg and cinnamon
1/8	tsp	EACH ginger, ground cloves, salt
3	md	fresh ripe peaches
½	c	raisins, if desired

Cream margarine or butter and sugar in a bowl. Add egg and beat until light and fluffy. In another bowl, mix flour, baking soda and seasonings. Stir flour mixture into egg mixture, a little at a time. Peel, pit and finely dice peaches; stir into cookie mixture. Stir in raisins, if desired. Drop dough, by rounded teaspoonsful, onto cookie sheet. Bake at 375⁰ for 20 minutes, until cookies are browned on top. Cool thoroughly on wire rack before storing.

Yield: about 4 dozen 2½-inch cookies.

Note: These are soft, cake-like cookies. If cookies become too soft on standing, put them into a warm 250⁰ to 300⁰ oven for a few minutes.

National Peach Council

SUMPTUOUS PEACH UPSIDE-DOWN CAKE
350°—45-50 Minutes

¼	c	soft butter or margarine
½	c	brown sugar (packed)
1½	c	canned sliced peaches, drained
6		maraschino cherries, halved
⅓	c	shortening
½	c	sugar
1		egg
1¼	c	sifted cake flour
1½	tsp	baking powder
1½	tsp	salt
½	tsp	grated orange rind
½	c	orange juice

Spread butter in bottom of 8-inch round cake pan and sprinkle with brown sugar. Arrange peaches and cherries on brown sugar. Cream the shortening and sugar in a bowl. Add the egg and beat well. Sift the flour, baking powder and salt together and add to creamed mixture alternately with mixture of orange rind and juice. Pour over peaches carefully. Bake at 350° for 45 to 50 minutes or until cake tests done. Cool for 10 minutes. Invert over serving plate and remove cake from cake pan.

Makes 6 to 8 servings.

SPICY PEACH UPSIDE DOWN CAKE
350° — 30 Minutes

2	c	chopped peaches
½	c	margarine or butter
¾	c	brown sugar
½	c	chopped pecans
1	pkg	spice cake mix

Sprinkle chopped peaches with lemon juice and sugar and set aside. Melt butter in 9x13-inch cake pan. Add brown sugar and pecans. Add layer of chopped peaches. Prepare cake mix according to package directions. Pour over peaches. Bake at 350° for 50 minutes or until done. Cool 10 minutes in pan, then invert onto serving tray. Serve with whipped topping or ice cream, if desired.

Georgia Peach Commission

POUND CAKE TOPPING

1½   tsp   cornstarch
1   can   (29 oz) sliced peaches, reserve syrup
2   tsp   lemon juice
¼   tsp   cinnamon
½   tsp   almond extract

Blend cornstarch and syrup from peaches. Add lemon juice, cinnamon and almond extract. Stir and cook until thickened. Add drained peach slices. Heat 3 minutes. Serve over pound cake.
Makes 8 servings.

South Carolina Peach Council

PEACH MELBA TOPPING FOR CHEESECAKE

1   pkg   (10 oz) frozen red raspberries, thawed
¼   c   currant jelly
1   T   cornstarch
1   can   (16 oz) sliced peaches

Reserve 2/3 cup syrup drained from raspberries. In small sauce pan, combine reserved syrup, currant jelly and cornstarch. Cook and stir until slightly thickened and glossy. Cool. Stir in raspberries. Drain peaches, top cake with peach slices and sauce.

CREAMY PEACH ICING

½	c	sliced peaches*
1	T	sugar
		Color keeper
1	pkg	(3 oz) cream cheese, softened
1	T	margarine or butter, softened
1	tsp	vanilla
2	c	powdered sugar
1		baked pound cake

Gently mix peaches with sugar and color keeper; cover and set aside. Blend cream cheese and margarine well. Add vanilla; beat in powdered sugar until mixture is smooth and creamy. Drain peaches, reserving liquid. Mash or finely chop peaches and stir into sugar-cream cheese mixture. Thin, if necessary with peach liquid. Spread over thoroughly cooled cake. For that "special" touch, add Festive Garnish.**

*When using frozen peaches, omit sugar and color keeper and be sure to drain thoroughly. If mixture is too thin, refrigerate or add more powdered sugar.

Festive Garnish: Gently mix 1 cup sliced peaches*, 2 tablespoons sugar and color keeper; cover and set aside. Cover iced cake completely with 1 package (7 ounce) coconut. Using peach slices as petals, make two large "flowers" in center of cake. Border with additional peach slices. Put 1 maraschino cherry in center of each flower.

***When using frozen peaches, omit sugar and color keeper and be sure to drain peaches thoroughly before using.

National Peach Council

FAVORITE PEACH SHORTCAKE

Filling:

4	c	fresh peeled, sliced peaches
⅓	c	sugar
		Stir together peaches and sugar; set aside.

Shortcake:

2	c	all-purpose flour
2	T	sugar
1	T	baking powder
½	tsp	salt
½	c	butter or margarine
1		egg, beaten
2/3	c	whole milk

Stir together flour, sugar, baking powder and salt. Cut in butter or margarine till mixture resembles coarse crumbs. Combine beaten egg and milk; add all at once to flour mixture. Stir just to moisten. Spread dough in greased 8x8x1½-inch baking pan; build up edges slightly. Bake 450° for 15 to 18 minutes (do not overbake). Cool in pan for 10 minutes. Remove from pan, split into 2 layers; carefully lift off top layer.

Topping:

1	c	whipping cream
2	T	sugar

Whip cream with sugar till stiff peaks form. Assemble cake by alternating layers of cake, filling, and whipped cream.

Makes 8 servings.

Just to work a little harder
For other people's good,
And to show a bit more friendship -
My friend, that's brotherhood.

Author Unknown

WALNUT-PEACH TORTE   325° — 30 Minutes

This torte is a true winner!

2/3	c	finely crushed vanilla wafers
½	c	ground walnuts (about 3 oz)
3	T	butter or margarine, softened
½	c	brown sugar, packed
1		egg
¾	c	all-purpose flour
¼	tsp	each baking soda and salt
½	c	whole milk
1	c	whipping cream
1	can	(7½ oz) peach slices, drained

Combine crushed vanilla wafers and ground nuts. Grease and flour one 8x1½-inch round baking pan. In small mixer bowl beat butter, brown sugar and egg with electric mixer till mixture is creamy. Stir together flour, baking soda and salt. Add to beaten mixture alternately with the milk, beating on low speed after each addition just till combined. Stir in the crumb mixture. Turn batter into prepared pan. Bake at 325° for 30 minutes or till cake tests done. Cool in pan 10 minutes. Remove from pan and cool on wire rack. Split cake layers in half horizontally. Cut each thin cake layer in half vertically, making four thin half-layers. To assemble, beat whipping cream with rotary beater to soft peaks. Place one half-layer of cake on a plate and spread with one-fourth of the whipped cream; top with second cake layer and spread with one-fourth of the whipped cream and arrange half the fruit atop. Complete torte in same pattern; chill till serving time. Cut into wedges to serve.

Makes 4 to 6 servings.

COCONUT PEACH TORTE   350°—25-30 Minutes

1	can	(29 oz) peach halves
3	T	butter or margarine
⅓	c	brown sugar
2/3	c	flaked coconut
1		1-layer pkg white cake mix
1	jar	peach sundae topping or make your own topping

Drain peach halves, reserving 3 tablespoons syrup. Melt butter or margarine in a saucepan; add reserved syrup and brown sugar. Pour into 5-cup ring mold. Sprinkle coconut over mixture. Prepare cake mix according to package directions and spoon over coconut. Bake in 350° oven for 25 to 30 minutes or till done. Cool 1 minute; invert on plate. Pile peach halves in center. Spoon peach sundae topping from jar over peaches. Serve cake while warm.

GREAT PEACH PUDDING CAKE 400°
15 Minutes + 30-35 Minutes

2	c	sifted all-purpose flour
2	T	granulated sugar
½	tsp	salt
¼	tsp	baking powder
½	c	butter or margarine
10		peach halves, fresh or canned
1	c	light brown sugar
1	tsp	cinnamon
2		egg yolks, slightly beaten
1	c	whipping cream

Sift flour, sugar, salt and baking powder together. Cut in butter till mixture resembles cornmeal; sprinkle over bottom and sides of greased 8x2-inch round ovenware cake dish. Place peaches, cut side up, over crumb mixture. Combine brown sugar and cinnamon; sprinkle over peaches. Bake at 400° for 15 minutes. Combine egg yolks and cream; pour over peaches, bake 30 to 35 minutes or till knife inserted comes out clean. Serve warm.

CREAM 'N PEACHES CAKE

1	pkg	butter-flavor cake mix
1½	c	sugar
4	T	cornstarch
4	c	chopped fresh peaches
½	c	water
2	c	whipping cream
2-3	T	powdered sugar
1	c	commercial sour cream
		Fresh sliced peaches

Prepare cake according to package directions, using two 8-inch cake pans. Cool and split each layer. Combine sugar and cornstarch in a saucepan. Add peaches and water; cook over medium heat, stirring constantly, until smooth and thickened. Cool mixture completely. Combine whipping cream and powdered sugar in a medium mixing bowl; beat until stiff peaks form. Spoon ⅓ of peach filling over split layer of cake; spread ⅓ cup sour cream over filling. Repeat procedure with remaining cake layers, peach filling and sour cream, ending with remaining cake layer. Frost with sweetened whipped cream, and garnish with fresh peach slices.

Yield: one 8-inch cake

COOK'S SPECIAL PEACH CAKE

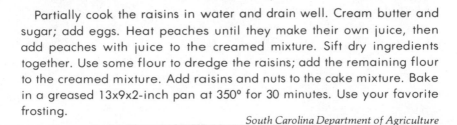

1	c	raisins
½	c	water
1	c	butter
1½	c	sugar
2		eggs
2	c	fresh peaches
2	c	all-purpose flour
2	tsp	soda
2	tsp	cocoa
1	tsp	each allspice, cinnamon and ground cloves
½	c	nuts

Partially cook the raisins in water and drain well. Cream butter and sugar; add eggs. Heat peaches until they make their own juice, then add peaches with juice to the creamed mixture. Sift dry ingredients together. Use some flour to dredge the raisins; add the remaining flour to the creamed mixture. Add raisins and nuts to the cake mixture. Bake in a greased 13x9x2-inch pan at 350° for 30 minutes. Use your favorite frosting.

South Carolina Department of Agriculture

FRESH PEACH OVENCAKE

450° — 15 Minutes
350° — 10-15 Minutes

3	T	butter or margarine
3		eggs
¾	c	whole milk
¾	c	flour
4	c	fresh sliced peaches
1	T	brown sugar
¾	c	dairy sour cream
2	T	maple syrup OR maple-flavored syrup

Put butter in 10- or 12-inch skillet with ovenproof handle. Place in 450° oven. In mixing bowl, beat eggs with rotary beater or wire whisk until light and lemon colored; beat in milk. Gradually stir in flour; beat until smooth. Remove skillet from oven; pour batter into skillet. Bake 15 minutes. Reduce oven heat to 350°. Continue baking 10 to 15 minutes until pancake is puffed and browned. While ovencake bakes, toss peaches with brown sugar; set aside. In separate bowl, mix sour cream with syrup. Serve hot ovencake topped with peaches and sour cream mixture.

Makes 4 to 6 servings.

California Tree Fruit Agreement

OVERNIGHT PEACH REFRIGERATOR CAKE

Impress your guests with this sensational cake!

½	lb	marshmallows
½	c	orange juice
½	c	ginger ale
1	c	whipped cream
		Sponge cake or lady fingers
6		to 8 peaches, sliced
½	c	chopped crystallized ginger

Cut marshmallows in quarters, add to orange juice and stir over hot water until almost melted; cool slightly and add ginger ale. When slightly thickened fold in ¾ **cup** whipped cream. Line a spring form pan with waxed paper. Arrange layer of cake or lady fingers on bottom, next a layer of ⅓ of the peaches, then layer ½ of the marshmallow filling; repeat until there are 3 layers of cake and 2 of filling. Chill in refrigerator overnight. Unmold; garnish with remaining peaches and whipped cream and chopped crystallized ginger. (Use fresh or canned peaches.)

Makes 6 to 8 servings. *Georgia Peach Commission*

CLASSIC SHORTCAKE WITH PEACH FILLING
450⁰ — 15-18 Minutes

An old family favorite!

2	c	packaged biscuit mix
2	T	sugar
1		egg, beaten
¼	c	butter or margarine, melted
2/3	c	whipping cream
		Peach Filling*

Combine biscuit mix, sugar, egg, butter and cream, mix well and beat vigorously 30 seconds. Spread dough in greased 8x1½-inch round pie pan, building up edges slightly. Bake at 450⁰ for 15 to 18 minutes or till done. Remove from pan; cool on rack 5 minutes. Place on serving plate. With serrated knife, split in 2 layers; lift top off carefully. Spread bottom layer with softened butter. Spoon Peach Filling between layers and atop. Cut in wedges - good when served warm.

*Peach Filling: Dip 1 quart fresh sliced peaches in color keeper; sweeten. Whip 1 cup whipping cream with 2 tablespoons brown sugar. Fold **half** of the peaches into **half** of the cream. Spread on bottom layer of shortcake. Cover top half of shortcake with remaining peaches and cream.

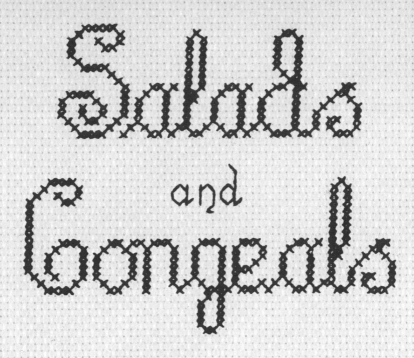

Salads and Congeals

Light and luscious salads and congeals begin with fresh peaches. Top them off with a variety of zesty salad dressings which lock in all the natural fresh flavor or dress them up with garnishes and serve them with pride. Salads and congeals can open a meal or close it; these can be prepared ahead, then served with delight by adding a spark to those special meals. Few dishes are more attractive as a main course of a luncheon or a part of a lavish buffet than a handsome molded peach salad. Many congeals are interchangeable as a salad or a dessert.

PEACH BOATS WITH SHRIMP SALAD

2	cans	(4½ oz ea) tiny shrimp
½	c	finely chopped celery
2	T	finely chopped green pepper
4	T	mayonnaise
1	tsp	lime juice
		Dash of EACH - onion salt, monosodium glutamate and worchestershire sauce
4	lg	peaches, peeled and halved
		Lettuce leaves

Drain shrimp and clean if necessary. Add celery and green pepper. Mix mayonnaise, lime juice and seasonings - add to shrimp. Mix well. Chill for at least an hour. Place peach halves on crisp lettuce leaves and spoon shrimp over the peaches.

Makes about 4 servings.

National Peach Council

GOURMET CHICKEN SALAD WITH FRESH PEACHES

A delicious luncheon main course.

2	c	chicken, cooked and cubed
¾	c	celery
¾	c	white seedless grapes
¾	c	fresh peeled and cubed peaches
½	c	mayonnaise
½	c	sour cream
		Seasoning salt to taste

Lightly toss chicken, celery, grapes and peaches together. Mix mayonnaise and sour cream and pour over salad. Add seasoning salt and mix gently. Store in refrigerator until ready to use. Garnish with fresh peach slices and parsley.

Makes 6 servings.

National Peach Council

PEACHY PICNIC SALAD

This salad will mark a special occasion for you.

1		bunch fresh spinach, trimmed, washed and dried
3	c	fresh peeled and sliced peaches, plums, nectarines and pears
1	c	shredded Swiss or Cheddar cheese
⅓	c	shelled nuts
		Peachy Cream Dressing*

Arrange spinach, fruits, cheese and nuts in salad bowl. Just before serving, pour dressing over; toss thoroughly. (If fruits are prepared early in the day, use commercial color keeper to prevent darkening.)

Makes 6 servings.

*Peachy Cream Dressing: Combine 1½ cups sliced peaches, ¼ cup dairy sour cream or plain yogurt, 1 tablespoon lemon juice, 1 tablespoon honey, ¼ teaspoon ginger and ¼ teaspoon salt into blender container and blend until smooth. Place in a covered container and refrigerate. Dressing will keep refrigerated up to 3 days. Use as salad dressing or as dessert sauce for sliced fruits.

Yields: about 1¼ cups dressing.

California Tree Fruit Agreement

CHICKEN FRUIT CURRY

Make it for family or for a special occasion.

4	med	peaches
2	c	cooked, cubed chicken
1	c	grapes, cut and seeded
1½	c	diced celery
2	T	diced green pepper
½	c	mayonnaise
¼	c	whipping cream
1	tsp	curry powder
1	T	chutney, optional
¼	tsp	salt
		Watercress or parsley

Peel and dice peaches; toss with chicken, grapes, celery and green pepper. Thin mayonnaise with whipping cream, stir in curry powder, chutney and salt. Pour dressing over chicken and fruit mixture. Toss together and chill. Garnish with watercress or parsley, if desired.

Makes 4 servings.

S.C. Department of Agriculture

PEACH SUPPER SALAD

2		fresh peaches, peeled and halved
2	tsp	lemon juice
		Romaine lettuce
1	c	cooked chicken, diced
2		green onions, sliced
¼	c	Curry Dressing*
2	med	tomatoes, peeled and chopped
2		hard-cooked eggs, chopped
2		slices crisply cooked bacon, crumbled
½		avocado, diced

Prepare peaches; sprinkle with lemon juice and set aside. Line large individual salad bowls with broken romaine leaves. Mix chicken and onion with enough dressing to moisten. Arrange peach halves in center of lettuce. Top with mound of chicken salad. Arrange remaining ingredients around peaches. Serve cold with extra Curry Dressing in pitcher.

Makes 2 servings.

*Curry Dressing:

Blend 1 cup sour cream or mayonnaise and ¼ cup milk. Stir in ½ teaspoon curry and ¼ teaspoon salt; add 2 teaspoons wine vinegar.

Yields: ½ cup dressing.

California Tree Fruit Agreement

FRUIT SALAD STRATA

Entertain guests with this fruit bowl salad.

2	c	shredded lettuce
*2	c	peaches, peeled and sliced
2	c	strawberries
*2	c	bananas, sliced
1	c	flavored yogurt
½	c	shredded Swiss cheese

Place **half** of the lettuce in bottom of large glass bowl. Top with layer of peaches, then layer of strawberries, then layer of bananas. Sprinkle remaining lettuce. Spread yogurt over top; sprinkle with shredded cheese. Cover and chill for several hours. Gently toss to serve.

Makes 12 servings.

*Use lemon juice to prevent browning.

SUMMER FRUIT SALAD

A refreshing fruit combination!

		Color Keeper
2	lg	applies, unpeeled and sliced
2		fresh nectarines, unpeeled and cut into wedges
2		fresh peaches, peeled and cut into wedges
1	can	(11 oz) mandarin oranges
1	can	(16 oz) pear halves, sliced
¼	c	sugar
1½	tsp	cornstarch
½		cantaloupe
1	c	seedless green grapes
		Maraschino cherries
		Fresh mint

Prepare color keeper solution according to manufacturer's directions. Toss apples, nectarines and peaches separately in prepared solution; drain fruit and set aside. Drain canned fruit and combine juices; stir well and set aside 1 cup of the fruit juice mixture. Combine sugar and cornstarch in a saucepan; stir in reserved fruit juice mixture. Cook over medium heat, stirring constantly, until mixture is thickened and bubbly. Scoop out melon balls, or peel melon and cut into cubes. Layer apples, mandarin oranges, grapes, cantaloupe, pears, nectarines and peaches in a 3-quart serving bowl; garnish with maraschino cherries and mint. Serve with fruit juice dressing.

Makes 10 to 12 servings.

FRESH PEACH CABBAGE SLAW

4	c	shredded cabbage
½	c	almonds
¼	c	raisins, optional
2	c	peeled and diced peaches
		Purchased cole slaw dressing
		OR
		Cottage Cheese Dressing*

Toss cabbage, almonds and raisins with dressing (if purchased dressing is used add 2 tablespoons sugar, if desired). Add peaches just before serving.

Makes 6 to 8 servings.

*Cottage Cheese Dressing: Combine 1 cup cottage cheese, ½ cup mayonnaise, 2 tablespoons honey, ¼ teaspoon celery seed, ¼ teaspoon monosodium glutemate, 1 teaspoon dry mustard and 1 tablespoon vinegar and mix well.

National Peach Council

PICK-UP PEACH SALADS

6		fresh peaches
		Juice of 1 lemon
2	pkgs	(3 oz each) cream cheese, softened
½	c	dairy sour cream
¼	c	chopped almonds or other nuts
¼	c	chopped dates
2	T	chopped crystallized ginger, optional
6		hot rolls

Wash thoroughly; halve and pit peaches but do not peel. Sprinkle with lemon juice to keep from darkening. Chill. Meanwhile, in small bowl, combine cream cheese, sour cream, almonds, dates and ginger. Spoon mixture into peach halves. Arrange on serving tray. Garnish with mint sprigs, if desired. Serve with napkins as "finger salad." Offer hot rolls to accompany peach salads.

Makes 6 servings, 2 halves per serving.

(Cream cheese mixture can be made the day before and refrigerated until needed.)

California Tree Fruit Agreement

CHEF'S CHOICE SALAD

Turn a casual get-together into a memorable meal.

⅓	c	honey
1	tsp	paprika
1	tsp	dry mustard
¼	tsp	salt
¼	c	white wine vinegar
½	c	salad oil
2	tsp	sesame seed, toasted
3	c	peeled and sliced peaches
6	c	torn mixed greens
2	c	cooked chicken or ham, cut into strips
1	c	American, Swiss, or brick cheese, cubed

In small mixer bowl combine honey, paprika, mustard and salt. Stir in vinegar. Add oil slowly; beating till thick. Beat in sesame seed. Fold in peaches. Cover and chill for several hours. To serve, arrange greens, cooked meat and cheese, and spoon fruit mixture over.

Makes 8 servings.

FLUFF PEACH SALAD

½	c	salad dressing
1	pkg	(3 oz) cream cheese, whipped
¼	c	nuts, chopped
¼	c	maraschino cherries, chopped
4		peaches, peeled and halved
		lettuce

Add salad dressing to cream cheese gradually; mix until blended. Stir in cherries and nuts; fill peach halves. Serve on lettuce.
Makes 8 servings.

South Carolina Peach Council

FROZEN FRESH PEACH SALAD

3	c	peeled and crushed fresh peaches
2	c	miniature marshmallows
½	c	drained crushed pineapple
½	c	(3 oz) slivered almonds
¼	c	(4 oz jar) maraschino cherries, quartered
½	tsp	almond extract
1/8	tsp	salt
2	c	sour cream
		Few drops red food coloring

Mix all ingredients in 2-quart bowl. Pour into 8-inch square pan or 12 muffin cups lined with paper baking cups. Cover with foil and freeze. Fifteen minutes before serving cut into squares or peel off paper cups.
Makes 12 servings.

S.C. Department of Agriculture

WALDORF PEACH SALAD

4	lg	unpeeled peaches
		orange juice
½	c	chopped celery
¼	c	chopped pecans
1	c	miniature marshmallows
		Mayonnaise

Wash peaches thoroughly and dice; mix lightly with a little orange juice to prevent darkening. Combine with celery, pecans and marshmallows. Top with mayonnaise. Serve in lettuce cups.

S.C. Department of Agriculture

GINGER PEACHY SALAD

For that special "company" lunch, double or triple as needed.

2	T	mayonnaise
1	tsp	lemon juice
1/8	tsp	ground ginger
1	can	chunk white chicken
½	c	chopped celery
⅓	c	green seedless grapes, cut in half
		Peach halves, drained
		Salad greens
		Toasted slivered almonds

In bowl, combine mayonnaise, lemon juice and ginger; toss with chicken, celery and grapes. Chill. Serve in peach halves arranged on salad greens. Garnish with almonds.

Yields: 1 cup salad.

CITRUS PEACH ASPIC

1	env	(1 T) unflavored gelatin
1½	c	water (¼ cold; 1¼ boiling)
2		pkgs (3 oz ea) peach flavored gelatin
1	c	orange juice
1		lemon (grate rind & 3 T juice)
1½	c	mashed fresh peaches
¼	c	sugar

Soften plain gelatin in ¼ **cup cold** water. Dissolve softened plain gelatin and peach flavored gelatin in 1½ cups hot water. Add orange juice, rind of lemon and lemon juice. Add mashed fresh peaches, sweeten to taste. Pour into 6-cup ring mold and chill until set. Serve with Cream Cheese Dressing: place 1 pkg (3 oz) cream cheese, softened, 1 tablespoon mayonnaise, and 1 peach, mashed, in mixing bowl. Beat until light and fluffy. Unmold aspic and fill center with Cream Cheese Dressing. Garnish with mint leaves if desired.

(For a nice change, substitute 1 package of lemon flavored gelatin for 1 package of peach flavored gelatin.)

PEACHES AND CREAM GELATIN SALAD

This colorful salad with golden fresh peaches as a garnish
will taste as good as it looks!

1st layer:

1	pkg	(3 oz) orange or peach flavored gelatin
1	c	boiling water
¾	c	cold water
3	c	sliced fresh peaches
1	sm	banana
½	med	apple, grated

Dissolve gelatin in the boiling water. Stir in cold water and chill till partially set. Fold in peaches, banana and apple. Pour into a 6-cup gelatin mold. Chill until nearly firm.

2nd layer:

1	env	(1 T) unflavored gelatin
3	T	cold water
½	c	light cream, scalded
1	pkg	(8 oz) cream cheese, softened
1	c	whipping cream, not whipped
½	c	sugar
1	c	pureed fresh peaches
2	T	sugar

Soften plain gelatin in 3 tablespoons cold water. Stir in scalded cream and mix till gelatin is dissolved. Cream together the softened cream cheese and whipping cream. Add the ½ cup sugar and mix thoroughly. Sweeten the pureed peaches with 2 tablespoons sugar and add to the cream cheese-whipping cream mixture. Combine with the dissolved gelatin and mix well. Pour over fruit gelatin layer in the mold and chill until firm. Unmold and garnish with peach slices to serve.

Makes 8 to 10 servings.

National Peach Council

PEACHY MELBA CROWN

1	pkg	(3 oz) raspberry flavor gelatin
2	c	water
1½	T	lemon juice, divided
1	env	unflavored gelatin
4		fresh peaches
½	c	sugar
1	c	dairy sour cream

In sauce pan over medium heat, dissolve raspberry flavored gelatin in **1¾ cups** water. Add ½ **tablespoon** of the lemon juice. Pour into 1½-quart mold. Chill until syrupy. Meanwhile in small saucepan, soften unflavored gelatin in ¼ **cup** water; then dissolve over low heat. Set aside. Halve and pit about 1½ peaches (unpeeled). Slice into blender container. Whirl smooth (there should be 1½ cups puree). Add dissolved gelatin, sugar, remaining **1 tablespoon** lemon juice and sour cream. Blend smooth. Slice remaining peaches (peeled, if desired). Stir into syrupy layer in mold. Pour sour cream mixture on top. Chill until firm. To serve; unmold onto platter, cut into wedges.

Makes 8 servings.

California Tree Fruit Agreement

God is the silent partner in all great enterprises.

Lincoln

JELLIED PEACH MELBA

2	pkgs	(3 oz ea) raspberry gelatin
2	c	boiling water
1	T	lemon juice
½	c	cold water
1	pkg	(10 oz) frozen peaches, slightly thawed
1	pkg	(10 oz) frozen raspberries, slightly thawed
1	pt	vanilla ice cream

Dissolve gelatin in boiling water. Add lemon juice and cold water. Add frozen fruit and stir gently until fruit thaws and separates - gelatin may begin to thicken. Pour into individual molds. Chill until firm. Just before serving, add a scoop of ice cream to each dish.

Makes 10 servings.

BAVARIAN PEACH CREAM

A traditional favorite.

1   pkg   (3 oz) peach-flavored gelatin
1   c   whipping cream, whipped
2   c   chopped fresh peaches

Prepare gelatin according to package directions; chill until the consistency of unbeaten egg white. Beat gelatin at high speed of electric mixer until foamy, about 2 to 3 minutes. Fold in whipped cream and peaches. Pour into a lightly oiled 6-cup mold. Cover and chill overnight. Unmold before serving.
Makes 6 to 8 servings.

ELEGANT PEACH BAVARIAN

1   can   (29 oz) sliced peaches
1   pkg   (3 oz) lemon gelatin
¼   c   sugar
           Dash of salt
1   c   boiling water
¼   tsp   almond extract
2   c   whipped topping

Drain peaches, reserving ⅓ cup of the syrup. Chop peaches. Dissolve gelatin, sugar and salt in boiling water. Add reserved syrup. Chill until slightly thickened. Blend almond extract into whipped topping; gradually blend into gelatin, then fold in the peaches. Pour into 5-cup mold. Chill until firm. Unmold.
Makes 10 servings.

BANANA PEACH DELIGHT

1   can   (16 oz) sliced peaches
1   pkg   (3 oz) orange-pineapple flavored gelatin
     OR
1   pkg   (3 oz) strawberry flavored gelatin
1   c   boiling water
1   banana, sliced

Drain peaches, measuring syrup. Add water to syrup to make 1 cup. Dissolve gelatin in boiling water. Add measured liquid. Pour into mold. Add peaches and banana. Chill until set.
Makes 8 servings.

YOGURT MOUSSE WITH FRESH PEACHES

1	pkg	(6 oz) lemon-flavor gelatin
2	c	boiling water
½	c	cold water
½	c	lemon juice
2		egg whites
2	T	sugar
¼	tsp	salt
1	ctn	(8 oz) plain yogurt
1	c	diced fresh peaches

Empty gelatin in a mixing bowl. Add 2 cups boiling water; stir until gelatin is dissolved. Add cold water and lemon juice; refrigerate until mixture is syrupy. In mixer bowl, beat egg whites until foamy; gradually beat in sugar and salt and continue beating until stiff peaks form. Add 1 cup of syrupy lemon gelatin mixture and yogurt to egg whites; blend well. Add peaches to remaining gelatin; then gently fold into egg white mixture. Spoon into a chilled 5-cup mold or pour into 8 small individual molds. Refrigerate until set. At serving time, unmold on serving platter or individual plates, garnish with crisp salad greens, if desired.

Makes 8 servings. (122 calories per serving when you use low-fat yogurt.)

California Tree Fruit Agreement

CREAMY PEACH MOLD

2	pkg	(3 oz ea) lime gelatin
¼	c	sugar
1/8	tsp	salt
2	c	boiling water
1	can	(16 oz) sliced peaches
1	T	lemon juice
2	pkg	(3 oz ea) cream cheese

Dissolve gelatin, sugar and salt in boiling water. Drain peaches, measuring syrup and adding water to make 1½ cups. Stir liquid and lemon juice into gelatin. Soften cream cheese; blend in 1 cup warm gelatin. Pour into 5-cup mold. Chill until set, but not firm. Chill remaining gelatin until slightly thickened. Stir in peaches, reserving a few for garnish. Spoon over set gelatin in mold. Chill until firm. Unmold. Garnish as desired.

Makes 8 to 10 servings.

SUNSHINE PEACH-BERRY MOLD

Summer comes to the Winter table!

1 pkg (3 oz) orange gelatin
1 c boiling water
1 can (16 oz) sliced peaches
1 pkg (10 oz) frozen raspberries

Dissolve gelatin in boiling water. Drain peaches, measuring syrup; add water to make ¾ cup. Stir into gelatin. Add frozen raspberries, separating berries with fork and stirring until mixture thickens. Then stir in peaches. Pour into serving dishes or a 1-quart serving bowl. Chill until firm. Garnish with sour cream, if desired.
Makes 6 servings.

SOUTHERN PICKLED PEACH SALAD

1 jar (29 oz) pickled peaches
1 pkg (6 oz) orange-flavored gelatin
1 c boiling water
1 pkg (8 oz) cream cheese, softened
1 can (8 oz) crushed pineapple, drained
 Lettuce leaves

Drain peaches, reserving 1 cup juice. Mash peaches with a fork; set aside. Dissolve gelatin in boiling water; add cream cheese, stirring until blended. Stir in reserved peach juice; chill salad until slightly thickened. Combine peaches and pineapple; add to gelatin mixture; stirring well. Pour into a lightly oiled 13x9x2-inch pan; chill until firm. Cut into rectangles; serve on lettuce leaves.
Makes 12 servings.

PICKLED PEACH SALAD

Salad with a zing!

1 jar (29 oz) pickled peaches
1 pkg (3 oz) lemon gelatin
1 c ginger ale
½ c chopped pecans

Measure 1 cup of syrup from pickled peaches, bring to a boil and pour over gelatin. Stir until gelatin dissolves. Add ginger ale and chill until slightly thickened. Add 1 cup chopped pickled peaches and pecans. Pour into a lightly oiled one-quart mold. Chill until set. Unmold and garnish, if desired.
Makes 8 servings.

Georgia Peach Commission

PICKLE-YOUR-OWN PEACH SALAD

½	c	sugar
½	c	light corn syrup
2	T	cider vinegar
1½	c	water
2		whole cloves
1	env	(1 T) unflavored gelatin
2	c	sliced peaches, drained

In a saucepan bring sugar, corn syrup, vinegar, **1 cup** water and cloves to a boil over high heat; then lower heat and simmer 20 minutes. Dissolve gelatin in **½ cup** cold water. Remove cloves from syrup mixture and add gelatin; stir until dissolved. Add peaches. Spoon into 4-ounce oiled molds; dividing fruit evenly. Refrigerate until set. Unmold and serve on lettuce leaf.

Makes 4 servings.

IMPERIAL PEACH DELUXE

A creative pleasure to make.

1	pkg	(3 oz) lime gelatin
2	c	boiling water
¾	c	cold water
1	can	(16 oz) peach halves
1	pkg	(3 oz) orange gelatin
1	pkg	(3 oz) cream cheese, softened
½	c	chopped pecans

Dissolve lime gelatin in **1 cup** boiling water. Add cold water. Pour about **half** the mixture into a 1½-quart ring mold. Chill until syrupy. Drain peaches, reserve syrup. Place peach halves, cut side up, in mold. Pour remaining lime gelatin over peaches. Chill until set, but not firm. Meanwhile, dissolve orange gelatin in **1 cup** boiling water. Blend in cheese, using rotary beater to blend thoroughly, if necessary. Add water to reserved peach syrup to make ¾ cup, if necessary; add to cheese mixture. Chill until very thick, then whip until fluffy. Add pecans. Spoon gently over set gelatin in the mold. Chill until firm. Unmold.

Makes 10 servings.

CREAM-TOPPED PEACHES

1	pkg	(3 oz) mixed fruit gelatin
2	T	sugar
1/8	tsp	salt
1	c	boiling water
1	can	(7½ oz) sliced peaches
2	tsp	lime or lemon juice
1	pkg	(3 oz) cream cheese, softened

Dissolve gelatin, sugar and salt in boiling water. Drain peaches, measuring syrup. Add water to make 1 cup. Stir syrup and lime juice into gelatin. Gradually blend ½ **cup** gelatin into cheese. Pour into an 8x4x2-inch loaf pan or a 1-quart mold. Chill until set, but not firm. Meanwhile, chill remaining gelatin until very thick. Stir in peaches; spoon into mold. Chill until firm. Cut in squares or unmold.

Makes 6 servings.

GEORGIA PEACH SALAD

2¼	c	orange juice, divided
1	pkg	(6 oz) orange-flavored gelatin
¼	c	plus 2 T sugar
1	tsp	grated lemon rind
2	c	buttermilk
1	c	coarsely chopped fresh peaches
1	c	fresh blueberries
		Lettuce
		Fresh peach slices, optional
		Fresh blueberries, optional
1	c	commercial sour cream

Bring **2 cups** orange juice to a boil in a medium saucepan. Add gelatin, sugar and lemon rind; stir until gelatin is dissolved. Chill until mixture is the consistency of unbeaten egg white. Gradually add buttermilk and mix well. Fold in 1 cup each peaches and blueberries. Pour mixture into a 6-cup mold; refrigerate until set. Unmold on lettuce-lined serving plate. Garnish with peach slices and blueberries, if desired. Combine sour cream and remaining ¼ cup orange juice; mix well and serve over salad.

Makes 10 to 12 servings.

CONGEALED SPICED PEACHES

1	can	(16 oz) sliced peaches
¼	c	vinegar
½	c	sugar
12		whole cloves
1/8	tsp	cinnamon
1	pkg	(3 oz) mixed fruit gelatin
¾	c	cold water

Drain peaches, measuring ¾ cup syrup. Chop peaches coarsely. Bring syrup, vinegar, sugar and spices slowly to a boil. Add peaches; simmer 10 minutes. Strain syrup and discard cloves. Add boiling water to hot syrup to make 1 cup, if necessary. Dissolve gelatin in hot syrup. Add cold water and peaches. Chill until firm. Unmold.

Makes 6 servings.

CHEESY PEACH SALAD

1	pkg	(3 oz) cherry gelatin
		Dash of salt
1	c	boiling water
¾	c	cold water
1¼	c	sliced peaches, fresh, canned or frozen*
1½	c	cottage cheese

Dissolve gelatin and salt in boiling water. Add cold water. Chill until very thick. Fold peaches into **1 cup** gelatin. Pour into a 1½-quart ring mold. Chill until set, but not firm. Beat cottage cheese until smooth. Whip remaining gelatin until fluffy. Fold in cheese. Pour into mold. Chill until firm. Unmold. If desired, fill ring with more cottage cheese and sliced peaches.

Makes 8 to 10 servings.

*If canned or frozen, drain thoroughly.

COLORFUL FRUIT SALAD

*This salad is especially good for outings
because the ingredients do not require refrigeration.*

1	can	(2l oz) apricot pie filling
1	can	(16 oz) sliced peaches, drained
1	can	(15 oz) pineapple chunks, drained
1	can	(11 oz) mandarin oranges, drained
4		bananas, sliced
1	c	maraschino cherries, optional

Combine all ingredients; toss gently. Cover and chill. Makes 8 to 10 servings.

CHICKEN 'N PEACHES SALAD

1	pkg	(12 oz) frozen rice pilaf*
½	c	mayonnaise
¼	c	chopped green pepper
2	T	sliced green onion
½	tsp	dried tarragon, crushed
2	c	cooked chicken, cubed
4		fresh peaches, peeled & sliced
		Lettuce

Prepare rice pilaf according to package directions; cool in mixing bowl. Stir in mayonnaise, green pepper, green onion, and tarragon. Add chicken; toss lightly to coat. Cover and chill. Shortly before serving, add peaches and toss. Serve in lettuce cups. *You may prefer making your own pilaf (pilau).
Makes 4 servings.

For nutrition, attractiveness, economy and taste, peaches are nature's perfect dessert! If the meal is light, select a heavy dessert; if the meal is heavy, serve a light dessert. Desserts with their infinite variety, offer the creative homemaker innumerable opportunities to climax her meals with a flourish of beauty as well as rich, smooth taste. Some peach desserts look so elegant and taste so delightful, they turn an ordinary meal into a festive occasion. Dessert peach sauces and toppings almost fall into the category of magic. With little effort, they can turn a simple cake or a bowl of peaches into a culinary triumph...or so it seems. There is an amazing variety of delightful chilled and frozen peach desserts—bombes, mousses, charlottes, etc. These recipes will bring warm words of praise from family and friends.

PEACH PUFF PUDDING   350°—45 Minutes

*An economical, tempting, easy to prepare dish, this pudding is
the kind that will have most people wanting second helpings.*

1½	c	whole milk
2	c	bread cubes
2	T	butter or margarine, melted
2		eggs, beaten
¼	c	honey
½	c	sugar
1/8	tsp	salt
¼	tsp	vanilla extract
1	tsp	grated lemon peel (dry peel can be used)
2	c	fresh diced peaches

Scald milk, pour over bread cubes. Let stand 10 minutes. Add melted
butter, beaten eggs, honey, sugar, salt, vanilla and lemon peel; mix
well and add peaches. Pour into a buttered 8x8x2-inch glass baking
dish. Bake at 350° for 45 minutes or until brown. Serve with milk, ice
cream or whipped topping.

Makes 4 to 6 servings.

National Peach Council

MACAROON FROZEN PEACH TORTE

2	c	mashed peaches
1	T	lemon juice
⅓	c	sugar
1	c	whipping cream, whipped
1	c	macaroon cookie crumbs

Combine the peaches, lemon juice and sugar in a bowl and mix well. Fold in whipped cream. Place half the crumbs in an 8-inch baking pan. Top with mixture and sprinkle crumbs on top. Freeze. Cut into squares to serve.

CHILLED PEACH SOUFFLE

A spectacular creation!

½	c	sugar
1	env	(1T) unflavored gelatin
¼	tsp	ground nutmeg
1/8	tsp	salt
½	c	water
4		egg yolks, beaten
1	T	lemon juice
½	tsp	vanilla
		Few drops almond extract
4	lg	fresh peaches
4		stiffly-beaten egg whites
½	c	whipping cream
		Toasted sliced almonds, optional

Combine sugar, gelatin, nutmeg and salt. Stir in water. Cook and stir over low heat till gelatin dissolves. Gradually stir hot mixture into beaten egg yolks. Return to saucepan; add lemon juice. Cook and stir till thickened. Remove from heat. Stir in vanilla and almond extract. Peel, pit and slice 2 of the peaches. Place sliced peaches in blender container and blend till finely chopped. Stir into gelatin mixture. Chill till partially set. Peel, pit and chop remaining 2 peaches. Fold into gelatin mixture. Fold in the stiffly-beaten egg whites. Whip cream; fold into gelatin. Chill till mixture mounds when dropped from spoon. Turn into a 1½-quart souffle dish. Chill till firm. Garnish with toasted, sliced almonds and peaches, if desired.
Makes 8 to 10 servings.

BAKED GINGER PEACHES   350°—15 Minutes

This recipe is never out of season.

1	can	(29 oz) peach halves
½	c	macaroon crumbs
½	tsp	ginger
1	c	whipping cream, whipped

Drain the peaches and reserve syrup. Place peaches in a greased shallow baking dish, cut side up. Mix crumbs and ginger with enough reserved peach syrup to moisten and fill peach centers with crumb mixture. Bake at 350° for 15 minutes and serve hot or cold with whipped cream.

GOLDEN PEACH FANTASIA

6		egg yolks
1¼	c	sugar
⅓	c	water
		Dash of salt
1	c	mashed peaches
1	pt	whipping cream
½	tsp	almond extract
½	tsp	vanilla extract

Beat the egg yolks well in top of double boiler and set aside. Combine **1 cup** sugar, water and salt in a 1-quart saucepan. Bring to a boil over low heat, stirring constantly, then cook, without stirring, to soft-boil stage. Beat syrup into egg yolks gradually and cook over simmering water, stirring constantly, until thickened. Cool and add peaches. Chill. Whip cream until soft peaks form. Add remaining ¼ cup sugar gradually and beat until stiff peaks form. Fold into peach mixture and add flavorings. Turn into deep mold. Freeze for 3 to 4 hours without stirring.

Makes 8 servings.

GLAZED PEACHES

1	can	(29 oz) peach halves
1		orange
1		lemon
		Whipped cream

Drain peaches. To the syrup add 2 teaspoons grated orange rind, 1 teaspoon grated lemon rind, then the juice of both orange and lemon. Simmer uncovered until the syrup is reduced to about **half.** Place fruit in syrup and poach gently for about 15 minutes, spooning the syrup over the fruit constantly. Be careful not to break the fruit. Pour into a bowl and chill. Serve with whipped cream which has been flavored with sugar and almond flavoring.

PEACH ICE CREAM BOMBE WITH RASPBERRY PUREE

A cool and refreshing dessert that's bound to please.

1	qt	peach ice cream*
2	c	sliced peaches
2	T	sugar
1	T	lemon juice
1	pkg	(10 oz) frozen raspberries, partially thawed
		Mint sprig, optional

*Peach Ice Cream: Add 1 cup chopped peaches flavored with ½ teaspoon almond extract to 1 quart slightly softened vanilla ice cream. Line 1-quart mold with plastic wrap, letting enough extend to wrap over top. Pack ice cream firmly into mold. Fold plastic wrap over ice cream; freeze until firm. Just before serving: toss 2 cups sliced peaches with sugar and lemon juice; set aside. Puree raspberries in blender or food processor or force through sieve. To serve, unmold ice cream onto chilled platter. Peel off plastic wrap. Surround the mold with peaches. Spoon some puree over ice cream and garnish with mint, if desired. Serve immediately with remaining puree.
Makes 8 servings.

CARDINAL PEACHES

Sheer elegance when served in crystal sherbet glasses!

6	c	water
2	c	sugar
2		slices lemon
2	T	vanilla extract
8	lg	peaches, firm ripe and peeled
		Raspberry Puree*

Combine water, sugar, lemon slices and vanilla in a large saucepan and bring to a boil; add peaches. When syrup returns to a simmering boil, test peaches with a toothpick. Remove from heat and cool in syrup. Drain peaches thoroughly and chill.

*Raspberry Puree: Add 2/3 cup sugar to 2 packages (10 ounce each) frozen raspberries, thawed, and puree in blender or food processor or force through a sieve. Chill.

When peaches and puree are thoroughly cold, arrange peaches in an oblong casserole and pour puree over and chill. Garnish with mint leaves, if desired.
Makes 8 servings.

REGAL PEACH MAHARANI

½	lb	small marshmallows
½	c	orange juice
½	c	ginger ale
1	c	whipping cream, whipped
½	c	chopped pecans
		Sliced sponge cake
8		peaches, peeled and sliced

Combine the marshmallows and orange juice in top of a double boiler and place over hot water. Stir until marshmallows are melted. Cool slightly and add ginger ale. Chill until thickened, then fold in whipped cream and pecans. Line a springform pan with waxed paper and place a layer of cake over waxed paper. Add half the peaches. Add half the marshmallow mixture and repeat layers. Chill overnight.

RASPBERRY PEACH PARFAIT

A winning combination - peaches and raspberries!

1½	c	chopped peaches
1½	T	sugar
1½	tsp	lemon juice
2	c	fresh raspberries
		OR
2	pkgs	(10 oz ea) frozen raspberries, thawed
1½	pts	vanilla ice cream
6		peach slices
6		whole raspberries

Place chopped peaches in a small bowl, sprinkle with sugar and lemon juice. Chill for ½ hour. Place raspberries (reserve 6) in a small bowl, mash with fork. Fill parfait glasses first with ice cream, alternating layers of peaches (reserve 6 slices), ice cream and raspberries. Place whole raspberry and peach slice on top of each parfait. Freeze. Allow to stand 15 minutes at room temperature before serving.

Makes 6 servings.

Optional Suggestion: Instead of parfait glasses you may use clear drinking glasses or clear glass 2-quart bowl. Alternate layers same as for parfaits.

Georgia Peach Commission

MARLOW PEACH FREEZE

1	c	crushed peaches
3	T	sugar
1	T	lemon juice
20		marshmallows
¼	c	water
½	pt	whipping cream, whipped

Sprinkle peaches with sugar and lemon juice and let stand. Combine marshmallows and water in a saucepan and cook over low heat, stirring occasionally, until melted. Add peaches and chill until thickened. Fold in whipped cream and pour into freezing tray. Freeze, without stirring, until firm.

Makes 6 servings.

GINGERED PEACH DELIGHT

1	can	peach pie filling
1	can	sweetened condensed milk
1	T	lemon juice
½	c	chopped pecans
2	T	chopped candied ginger
1½	c	whipping cream, whipped

Combine the pie filling and milk in a bowl and beat with electric mixer until peaches are crushed. Mix in lemon juice, pecans and candied ginger, then fold in whipped cream. Pour into ice cube trays and freeze until firm. Serve in parfait glasses.

CREAMY PEACH FREEZE

1	pkg	(1¼ oz) whipped topping mix
1	can	(16 oz) sliced peaches, drained

Prepare whipped topping mix according to package directions. Combine whipped topping and peaches in container of electric blender; process until smooth. Spoon into 4 serving dishes; freeze 2 to 3 hours or until firm. Remove from freezer 5 minutes before serving.

Makes 4 servings.

BERRY-PEACH COMPOTE

Serve in stemmed glasses for a very special occasion.

6	lg	peaches, peeled and sliced
1	T	lemon juice
1	pt	fresh raspberries or blueberries
⅓	c	sugar
1	c	whipping cream, whipped
1/8	tsp	ground ginger
1/8	tsp	ground nutmeg

Combine peaches and lemon juice; mix well. Add berries; sprinkle with sugar. Let stand until sugar dissolves. Mix well, and spoon into individual serving dishes. Top with whipped cream. Combine ginger and nutmeg, mix well and sprinkle over whipped cream.

Makes 6 to 8 servings.

UNLAYERED PEACH PARFAIT

1	T	plus 1 tsp. unflavored gelatin
½	c	cold water
½	c	sugar
1	can	(12 oz) peach nectar
2	T	water
1	T	lemon juice
4	med	peaches, peeled and cut up
		Whipped Topping, optional
		Additional Peach slices, optional

Dissolve gelatin in ½ cup cold water; bring to a boil, stirring constantly. Remove from heat; stir in sugar and peach nectar. Chill until consistency of unbeaten egg white. Combine 2 tablespoons water and lemon juice in a medium bowl; add 4 peaches, tossing gently to coat. Drain peaches, and combine with thickened nectar mixture; spoon evenly into 6 parfait glasses. Chill until firm. Just before serving, top each parfait with whipped topping and an additional peach slice, if desired.

Yield: 6 parfaits.

FRUIT 'N CREAM SUPREME

Highlight your next occasion with this party-special delight.

1	can	(14 oz) condensed milk
⅓	c	lemon juice
1	c	(8 oz) sour cream
1	tsp	vanilla OR almond extract
1	can	(21 oz) peach pie filling
	OR	
4	c	fresh or canned peaches, well drained

In medium bowl, combine condensed milk and lemon juice; mix well. Stir in sour cream and extract. Layer cream mixture and peaches in dessert glasses, topping with peaches. Chill 30 minutes in freezer or 2 hours in refrigerator. Refrigerate leftovers.

Makes 6 to 8 servings.

FRUITY TOPPED DESSERT

1½	c	apple juice
¼	c	honey
4		peaches, peeled and sliced
2		bananas, peeled and sliced
1	c	pitted dark sweet cherries, halved
		vanilla ice cream

Combine apple juice and honey in a medium saucepan; stir well. Bring to a boil; reduce heat and cook, stirring occasionally, until mixture is reduced by about one-third. Stir in fruit; simmer 5 minutes or until fruit is thoroughly heated. Serve over vanilla ice cream.

Makes about 1 quart.

DAINTY PEACH FAVORITE

2	c	pureed fresh peaches
½	c	sugar
1	tsp	lemon juice
		Dash of salt
2	c	whipped topping

Combine peaches, sugar, lemon juice and salt; stir well. Fold in whipped topping. Chill until serving time. Serve with thin wafers or lightly flavored cookies.

Makes about 4 cups.

BLUSHING PEACH COMPOTE

Add zest and color with cinnamon candies.

8	lg	ripe peaches
2	c	water
⅓	c	lemon juice
1	c	orange juice
½	c	sugar
2	T	red cinnamon candies
12		whole cloves

Peel, halve and pit peaches. Combine water, lemon juice, orange juice, sugar, cinnamon candies and cloves in a large saucepan. Add peach halves and simmer 10 minutes, or until peaches are easily pierced. Cool peach halves in syrup. Chill. Serve with cookies or light cake.

Makes 8 servings.

California Tree Fruit Agreement

QUICK AND EASY PEACH DESSERT   350°—45 Minutes

½	c	margarine
½	c	brown sugar
¾	c	flour
1	tsp	cinnamon
6-8		peaches, peeled & sliced

Blend margarine with sugar, flour and cinnamon. Place over peaches in buttered 6x10x2-inch baking dish. Bake at 350° for 45 minutes or until crisp and brown. Cool; serve with whipped cream, if desired.

Makes 6 to 8 servings.

CHILLED PEACH MIETTE

4	c	peeled and sliced fresh peaches
½	c	brown sugar, packed
¾	c	graham cracker crumbs
		Whipped cream or ice cream

Place the peaches in a shallow dish. Mix the sugar with crumbs and sprinkle over peaches. Toss lightly and chill. Top with whipped cream and serve.

Makes 4 to 6 servings.

PEANUT-PEACH DUMPLING SURPRISE

3	c	buttermilk biscuit mix
⅓	c	peanut butter
1	can	(14 oz) sweetened condensed milk
1	tsp	grated orange rind
2	c	orange juice
1	can	(29 oz) peach slices, undrained
¼	c	butter or margarine

Mix biscuit mix and peanut butter until crumbly. Stir in condensed milk and orange rind. Shape mixture into 12 balls. In a Dutch oven combine orange juice, undrained peach slices and butter. Bring mixture to a boil. Add dough balls. Cover and lower heat and simmer for 15 minutes or until balls are puffed. Serve dumplings with peach slices and juice spooned over them. Serve hot, plain or topped with ice cream and chopped peanuts.

Makes 8 to 12 servings.

South Carolina Peach Council

All that I have seen teaches me to trust the Creator for what I have not seen.

Author Unknown

PEACH FILLING FOR SHORTBREADS

8		ripe peaches, peeled and sliced
		Water to cover
1/8	tsp	salt
2½	T	lemon juice
¼	c	butter or margarine
2	tsp	cornstarch
2/3	c	sugar
		Shortbread
		Whipped cream

In a saucepan cover peaches with water and add salt, lemon juice and butter. Cook over medium heat and bring to a simmering boil. Add cornstarch and sugar and cook until thickened. Arrange single shortbread on dessert plate and cover with some of peaches with syrup and top with whipped cream.

Makes 8 servings.

FAMILY STYLE PEACHES 'N CREAM

½	box	graham crackers
1	can	(29 oz) sliced peaches, diced
½	pt	whipping cream, whipped
3	T	sugar

Use deep 2-quart casserole dish. Break double graham crackers in half; line bottom and sides of dish. Layer undrained diced peach slices on crackers; cover with whipped cream sweetened with sugar. Continue layers twice, ending with whipped cream. Garnish with peach slices; chill at least 2 hours before serving.
Makes 6 servings.

South Carolina Peach Council

Our aim should be to do each day something worthy, some noble deed in kindness which brings joy and gladness to our fellowman, for this brings us a step nearer to God.

Unis

DESSERT SUPREME

For a delicious, easy-to-make dessert, mix sliced fresh peaches with sour cream and confectioner's sugar to taste, Flavor with vanilla extract and chill thoroughly before serving.

S.C. Department of Agriculture

GLAMOROUS PEACH MELBA

Place peeled peach half in dessert dish. Put a scoop of vanilla ice cream on peach half. Pour crushed raspberries on top, or use raspberry jam, warmed to thin it.

Try all three, then pick your favorite!

Peache Mousse #1

2	c	peeled and sliced peaches
2/3	c	sugar
2	c	whipping cream, whipped
		Almond extract

Cover the peaches with sugar and let stand for 1 hour. Press through a sieve. Fold in whipped cream and almond extract and pour into a mold. Freeze.

Makes 10 to 12 servings.

Peach Mousse #2

1	c	peeled and chopped peaches
6	tsp	sugar
1	c	whipping cream, whipped
2		egg whites, lightly beaten
		Dash of salt

Mix peaches and **4 tablespoons** sugar and fold into whipped cream. Add remaining 2 tablespoons sugar and salt to egg whites and beat until soft peaks form. Fold into peach mixture and pour into mold. Freeze until firm.

Makes 6 to 8 servings.

Peach Mousse #3

1	env	(1 T) unflavored gelatin
¼	c	cold water
2	T	lemon juice
1	c	sugar
1	c	peeled and mashed peaches
2	c	whipping cream, whipped

Soften the gelatin in the cold water and dissolve over boiling water. Place in a bowl and stir in the lemon juice, sugar and peaches. Chill until thickened. Fold in the whipped cream and chill until firm.

Makes 6 servings.

Preserves

From the garden to the jar, preserving is the best way to bring your summer garden to your winter table. You're at your creative best when making jams, marmalades and all their variations. Plan ahead during peach season and pack flavorful peach products in heatproof glasses suitable for gift-giving; tie a ribbon around a jar of peach preserves and let it say welcome to a new neighbor or express your appreciation to special friends by presenting them with a jar of homemade peach pickles or chutney, especially for those who are not lucky enough to live in "peach land." For a rewarding, uncomplicated and creative experience to use at home or share, have fun with the many variations of jellying!

Preserving Peaches

JELLY is made from fruit juice without any pieces of fruit. It is clear, shimmering, and quite firm, yet tender.

MARMALADE is a jelly with pieces of fruit suspended in the transparent jelly.

JAM is made from crushed or ground whole fruit cooked with sugar until the mixture is homogeneous, smooth and thick, and has the natural color and flavor of the fruit from which it is made.

CONSERVE is a jamlike product made from a mixture of several fruits. At least one citrus fruit is usually included. A true conserve contains nuts and raisins.

PRESERVES are fruits preserved with sugar so that the fruit retains its shape and is clear and shiny, tender and plump.

FRUIT BUTTERS are made by cooking fruit pulp with sugar to a thick consistency which will spread easily. Spices may be added to suit personal taste.

FRUIT PICKLES are whole or pieces of fruit cut into uniform and attractive sizes and shapes, and will have a better flavor and be more plump if left standing in the syrup for several hours after cooking and then pickled and processed.

CHUTNEY is a condiment of fruits seasoned with herbs and spices, usually containing raisins and onions.

Several ingredients are common to jellies, jams, etc. These are (1) fruit, (2) sugar, (3) pectin, and (4) usually an acid.

(1) **Fruit** provides the sought-after flavor.

(2) **Sugar** is important for three reasons: it acts as a preservative, develops the flavor by adding sweetness, and aids in the formation of the gel.

(3) **Pectin** is a water soluble carbohydrate which is responsible for making the jelly gel. It is naturally present in fruits, but the amounts vary. Slightly underripe fruit contains more pectin than does completely ripe fruit. Commercial fruit pectin in dry and liquid forms can be added to fruits in order to produce a firmer jam, jelly or preserve. The addition of commercial pectin eliminates the need for long-cooking to concentrate a jam to the point of proper consistency.

(4) **Acid** is needed for flavor and for the gel formation. The acid content varies in different fruits and with fruits that are low in acid, lemon juice or citric acid is commonly added.

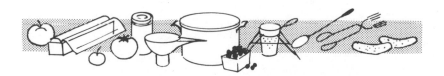

PEACH-ORANGE MARMALADE WITH WALNUTS

12	md	peaches
2-3	md	oranges, seeds removed
6	c	sugar
1	jar	(16 oz) maraschino cherries
1	c	coarsely chopped walnuts or pecans

Peel and slice peaches. Grind oranges, including rinds, in food chopper (or chop in electric blender). Put peaches and oranges into 6- to 8-quart kettle. Add sugar and let stand 15 to 20 minutes to let juices form. Bring to boil over medium heat, lower heat and simmer slowly, until fruit and liquid are clear and mixture reaches desired thickness, about 2 hours. Stir frequently to prevent mixture from sticking and burning. Cut cherries in half and add, with juice, to peach-orange mixture. Stir in nuts and simmer 5 minutes. Remove from heat. Ladle into hot jars and seal with self-sealing lids or paraffin.

Yield: 10 half-pints.

National Peach Council

FREEZER SPICED PEACH JAM

2	lbs	fully ripe peaches
2	T	lemon juice
1	tsp	ascorbic acid crystals
½	tsp	EACH ground ginger and ground nutmeg
4	c	sugar
1	c	light corn syrup
¾	c	water
1	pkg	(1¾ oz) powdered fruit pectin

Peel and finely chop peaches using fine blade of food grinder, blender or food processor. Measure 2¼ cups (if necessary add water to make exact measure) into a 4-quart bowl. Add lemon juice and ascorbic acid; stir well. Add ginger and nutmeg; stir well. Add sugar and corn syrup, stirring thoroughly to dissolve sugar. Let stand 10 minutes. In small saucepan mix water and fruit pectin. Stirring constantly, bring to boil over medium heat and boil 1 minute. Pour into fruit mixture. Stir vigorously 3 minutes. (A few sugar crystals will remain.) Ladle into freezer containers leaving ½-inch headspace (no paraffin needed). Cover with tight lids. Let stand at room temperature until set - it may take up to 24 hours. Store in refrigerator if to be used within a week or two or freeze for later use.

Yield: 7 half-pints.

Georgia Peach Commission

FREEZER PEACH STRAWBERRY JAM

1½	lbs	fully ripe peaches
¼	tsp	ascorbic acid crystals
1	pt	strawberries
5½	c	sugar
1	c	light corn syrup
2		pouches (3 oz ea) liquid fruit pectin
⅓	c	lemon juice

Peel, pit and thinly slice peaches. Crush peaches, one layer at a time, to let juice flow freely. Measure 1¾ cups; stir in ascorbic acid. Hull strawberries, fully crush, one layer at a time, to let juice flow freely. Measure 1 cup. In large bowl stir together fruit, sugar and corn syrup until well blended; let stand 10 minutes. In small bowl mix pectin and lemon juice. Stir into fruit mixture. Stir vigorously 3 minutes. Ladle into freezer containers leaving ½-inch headspace (no paraffin needed). Cover with tight lids; let stand at room temperature until set. Jam to be eaten within a week or two may be stored in refrigerator. Freeze remaining containers and transfer to refrigerator as needed.

Yield: 8 half-pints.

FREEZER PEACH JAM

4	c	peeled, crushed fresh peaches
¼	c	lemon juice
1	pkg	(1¾ oz) powdered fruit pectin
1	c	light corn syrup
5½	c	sugar

Measure peaches into large kettle and add lemon juice. While stirring, slowly add pectin. Let stand 20 minutes; stir every 5 minutes to blend pectin with fruit. Add syrup and blend well; add sugar and blend well. Cook over low heat until just warm to the touch (about 100°F). Do not allow mixture to become hot. Pour jam into jars to within ½-inch from top. Cover jars at once. Let stand until "jellied". Store in freezer until ready to use. Keep in refrigerator once jar has been opened.

Yield: 8 half-pints.

National Peach Council

FREEZER PEACH JAM
(using powdered fruit pectin)

2¼	c	peeled chopped or ground peaches
2	T	lemon juice
5	c	sugar
¾	c	water
1	pkg	(¾ oz) powdered fruit pectin

Combine chopped peaches and lemon juice. Thoroughly mix sugar into fruit, and let stand for 10 minutes. Mix water and fruit pectin in a small saucepan. Boil 1 minute, stirring constantly. Stir into the fruit, and continue stirring about 3 minutes. Ladle jam into scalded jars or plastic containers; leave room for expansion. Cover right away and let stand at room temperature for 24 hours to set. Keep in refrigerator or freezer.

Yield: 5 half-pints.

FREEZER PEACH JAM

1	c	pureed peaches
2¾	c	sugar
½	c	light corn syrup
½	tsp	ascorbic acid powder
1	pkg	(3 oz) liquid fruit pectin
1	T	lemon juice

   To peaches add sugar, corn syrup and ascorbic acid powder and blend thoroughly. Allow to stand 10 minutes. Add pectin and lemon juice and blend well. Pour into freezer containers leaving ½-inch headspace. Cover with tight fitting lids. Let stand at room temperature 24 hours or until set. Place in freezer. (This jam does not freeze solidly and may be used directly from the freezer.) Jam can be stored up to two weeks in the refrigerator.
   Yield: about 4 cups.

Georgia Peach Commission

In the hurried pace of life today
So much is missed along the way...
Take time to notice the wondrous things
Of God's creation, the eternal things.

Gladys Billings Bratton

FREEZER PEACH JAM
(using liquid fruit pectin)

2½	lbs	fully ripe peaches
1	tsp	ascorbic acid crystals
6½	c	sugar
2		pouches (3 oz ea) liquid fruit pectin
⅓	c	lemon juice

   Peel, pit and finely chop peaches. Measure 3 cups and combine with ascorbic acid crystals in a large bowl. Stir in sugar; let stand 10 minutes. Combine pectin and lemon juice; stir into peaches. Keep stirring 3 to 4 minutes; until sugar is dissolved. Ladle jam into sterilized jars, filling to within 1-inch of tops to allow for expansion in freezing. Wipe rims and cover jars with lids; screw bands on tightly. Let stand at room temperature until jam thickens, usually about 24 hours. Store in refrigerator for up to 3 months or in the freezer for up to 1 year.
   Yield: 7 half-pints.

OLD FASHION PEACH PICKLES

24	sm	firm-ripe peaches
1		piece ginger root
2		sticks cinnamon
1	T	whole allspice
1	T	whole cloves
5-6	c	sugar
2	c	water
3	c	vinegar

Wash and peel peaches and drop into a cold salt and vinegar water solution (2 tablespoons each of salt and vinegar per gallon of water). Tie spices in a cheesecloth bag. Add spice bag, **2 cups** sugar and water to vinegar. Bring to boiling. Wash salt and vinegar water off peaches and drain well. Add peaches, a few at a time; simmer until heated thoroughly. Carefully remove peaches. Repeat until all peaches have been heated. Pour boiling syrup over peaches; cover and let stand 3 to 4 hours. Carefully remove peaches from syrup. Add **2 cups** sugar to the syrup and heat to boiling. Pour over peaches; cover and let stand 12 to 18 hours in a cool place. Pack peaches into hot sterilized jars, leaving ½-inch headspace. Add remaining **1 to 2 cups** sugar to syrup. Bring to boiling; pour over peaches, leaving ¼-inch headspace. Adjust lids and process pints and quarts 15 minutes in boiling water bath.

Yield: about 6 pints.

PICNIC PEACH PICKLE

8	lbs	small or medium-size peaches
2	T	whole cloves
4		two-inch stick cinnamon
2	lbs	sugar
1	qt	vinegar

Wash and peel peaches. Put cloves and cinnamon loosely in a clean, thin, white cloth and tie top tightly. Cook together spices, sugar and vinegar for 10 minutes. Add peaches; cook slowly until tender, but not broken. Let stand overnight. In the morning remove spices. Drain syrup from peaches; boil syrup rapidly until thickened. Pack peaches in clean, hot sterilized jars. Pour hot syrup over peaches, filling jars to top. Seal tightly. Process in water bath at simmering temperature (about 180°) for 10 minutes.

SPICED PEACHES

5	c	sugar
1	c	vinegar
12	in	stick cinnamon, broken
2	tsp	whole cloves
2	c	water
5	lbs	small peaches

Combine sugar, vinegar, cinnamon, cloves and water. Bring to boiling; reduce heat. Peel peaches. (If desired, halve and pit.) To prevent darkening, add peaches to syrup as soon as they are peeled. Simmer about 5 minutes. Remove from heat. Spoon peaches into hot, sterilized jars, leaving ½ inch headspace. Return syrup to boiling and add to peaches to cover, leaving ½ inch headspace. Wipe rims; adjust lids. Process in boiling water bath for 20 minutes.

Yield: 5 or 6 pints.

To live is not to live for one's self alone; let us help one another.

Menander

CALIFORNIA SPICED PEACHES

5-7	lbs	fresh peaches
2	c	brown sugar, packed
1	c	honey
1	c	water
½	c	white vinegar
		sticks (2 inches each) cinnamon

Remove skins, cut in half and pit peaches. Place peaches into 1 quart cold water into which 1½ teaspoons **each** salt and vinegar have been mixed. Combine brown sugar, honey, water, vinegar and cinnamon in large saucepan. Simmer 10 minutes, stirring occasionally until sugar dissolves. Drain half the peaches, add to syrup and simmer 5 minutes, spooning syrup over peaches. Pack into clean, hot jars; add syrup to ½-inch of top. Repeat with remaining peaches. Adjust lids and set jars on rack in canning pot and add boiling water to cover jars by 1 to 2 inches. Bring water back to a boil and process 20 minutes. Remove from water bath at once and set on heat-proof surface until cold before storing.

Yield: 5 pints.

California Tree Fruit Agreement

SPICED PEACH BUTTER

8	c	crushed or blended peaches
4	c	sugar
1/8		to ¼ t salt
1	tsp	cinnamon
½	tsp	ginger
½	tsp	allspice

Mix peaches, sugar and salt in a large kettle. Boil rapidly, stirring constantly to prevent scorching. As the butter becomes thick, lower heat to reduce spattering. Add spices. Continue cooking until butter is thick enough to almost flake off the spoon. Pour into hot sterilized jars to within ½ inch of top. Adjust lids and process 10 minutes in boiling water bath at simmering temperature (180°-185°).

Yield: about 8 half-pints.

National Peach Council

PEACH BUTTER

2	qts	pureed peaches
4	c	sugar

Peel and puree peaches in a blender, or cook peaches until soft and run through a food mill. Measure puree. Add sugar and cook until thick, about 30 minutes. Stir frequently to prevent sticking. Pour into hot jars, adjust caps and process 10 minutes in boiling water bath.

Yield: about 4 pints.

Spiced Peach Butter
Add ½ - 1 teaspoon each of ground ginger and ground nutmeg along with the sugar and process as above.

Georgia Peach Commission

OLD FASHION PEACH PRESERVES

| 2 | qts | sliced peaches |
| 6 | c | sugar |

Combine fruit and sugar and allow to stand 12-18 hours in the refrigerator. Slowly bring to a boil and cook gently until the fruit becomes clear and the syrup thickens, about 40 minutes. Stir frequently to prevent sticking. Skim if necessary. Pour boiling hot into hot canning jars. Adjust caps and process in boiling water bath 15 minutes. This recipe may be halved or doubled as desired.

Yield: about 7½ half pints.

Georgia Peach Commission

EASY PEACH PRESERVES

A favorite for family and friends to enjoy year-round.

3½	c	sugar
2	c	water
5	c	peeled sliced peaches

Combine sugar and water in a large saucepot; cook over medium heat, stirring constantly, until sugar dissolves. Add peaches, and bring to a boil. Cook 20 minutes or until peaches are clear, stirring occasionally. Remove from heat; cover and let stand 12 to 18 hours in a cool place. Drain peaches, reserving liquid in pan. Spoon peaches into hot sterilized jars; set aside. Bring liquid to a boil. Cook 2 to 3 minutes, stirring often; pour liquid over peaches, leaving ¼-inch headspace. Cover at once with metal lids and screw metal bands tight. Process in a boiling-water bath 15 minutes.

Yield: 6 half-pints.

Note: If desired, one of the following may be added just before preserves are removed from heat:

2		cracked peach pits
2		drops almond
½	c	sliced maraschino cherries
½	tsp	ground ginger, nutmeg OR cloves

Add zip to your meal with your choice of chutney.

"JELLED" PEACH CHUTNEY

3	lbs	peaches
½	c	vinegar
¼	c	lemon juice
1	c	seedless raisins
¼	c	slivered drained preserved ginger
⅓	c	chopped onion
1	T	salt
1	tsp	ground allspice
½	tsp	EACH ground cinnamon, cloves, and ginger
¾	c	firmly packed dark brown sugar
4½	c	granulated sugar
1	box	(1¾ oz) powdered pectin

Peel and pit fully ripe peaches. Cut in small pieces. Measure 4 cups into a very large saucepan. Add vinegar, lemon juice, raisins, slivered ginger, onion, salt, allspice, cinnamon, cloves and ground ginger; mix thoroughly. Measure sugars; set aside. Add pectin to fruit; mix well. Place over high heat; stir until mixture comes to a hard boil. At once stir in sugars. Bring to a full rolling boil and boil hard 5 minutes; stirring constantly. Remove from heat; skim off foam with metal spoon. Stir and skim for 10 minutes to cool slightly and prevent floating fruit. Ladle quickly into glasses. Cover at once with 1/8 inch hot paraffin.
     Yield: about 10 half-pints.

HOLIDAY PEACH CHUTNEY

4	qts	peeled and finely chopped peaches
1	c	seedless raisins
1	c	chopped onions
2-3	c	brown sugar
2	T	ground ginger
¼	c	mustard seed
2	tsp	salt
1		clove garlic, minced, optional
1		hot red pepper
5	c	vinegar

Combine all ingredients and cook slowly until thick, about 40 minutes. Stir frequently to prevent sticking. Pour, boiling hot, into hot pint jars, leaving ¼-inch headspace. Adjust lids and process in boiling water bath 10 minutes.
     Yield: about 7 pints.

These freezer jams have a light, fresh, fruity taste!

FREEZER PEACH RASPBERRY JAM
(using liquid fruit pectin)

1	lb	fully ripe peaches
1½	c	fully ripe raspberries
3	c	sugar
1	c	light corn syrup
1		pouch (3 oz) liquid fruit pectin
2	T	lemon juice

Peel, pit and thinly slice peaches. Crush peaches, one layer at a time, to let juice flow freely. Measure 1 cup. Fully crush raspberries, one layer at a time, to let juice flow freely. Measure 1 cup. In large bowl stir together fruit, sugar and corn syrup until well blended. Let stand 10 minutes. In small bowl mix pectin and lemon juice. Stir into fruit mixture. Stir vigorously 3 minutes. Ladle into freezer containers leaving ½-inch hadspace (no paraffin needed). Cover with tight lids. Let stand at room temperature until set. Jam to be eaten within a week or two may be stored in refrigerator. Freeze remaining containers; transfer to refrigerator as needed.

Yield: 5 half-pints.

FREEZER PEACH RASPBERRY JAM
(using powdered fruit pectin)

1¼	lbs	peaches
2	T	lemon juice
1	pt	raspberries
5	c	sugar
¾	c	water
1	box	(1¾ oz) powdered fruit pectin

Peel, pit and finely chop fully ripe peaches. Measure 1¼ cups into a large bowl or pan. Add the lemon juice. Thoroughly crush, a layer at a time, about 1 pint fully ripe red raspberries; measure 1 cup into the bowl. Add sugar to fruits; mix well. Mix water and pectin in small saucepan, bring to a boil and boil 1 minute, stirring constantly. Stir into fruits. Continue stirring about 2 minutes. (A few sugar crystals will remain.) Quickly ladle into freezer containers, allowing space for expansion; cover with tight lids. Let stand until set - about 24 hours; store in freezer. For use within 2 to 3 weeks, store in refrigerator.

Yield: about 6 half-pints.

*Tasty fruit combinations are captured
in these conserves.*

CALICO PEACH-PINEAPPLE CONSERVE

A panorama of colorful fruit!

2½	lbs	peaches
⅓	c	chopped maraschino cherries
1	can	(8½ oz) crushed pineapple
¼	c	lemon juice
1½	c	chopped nuts
7½	c	sugar
1	btl	(6 oz) liquid pectin

Peel and pit fully ripe peaches; chop very fine or grind. Measure 2¼ cups into very large saucepan. Add cherries, pineapple, lemon juice and nuts. Add sugar to fruit; mix well. Place over high heat; bring to a full rolling boil and boil hard 1 minute, stirring constantly. Remove from heat and at once stir in liquid pectin. Skim off foam. Stir and skim for 5 minutes to cool slightly and prevent floating fruit. Ladle quickly into sterilized jars. Cover with 1/8 inch hot paraffin.
Yield: about 10 to 12 half-pints.

CANTALOUPE-PEACH CONSERVE

3	c	peeled chopped peaches
3	c	chopped cantaloupe
4¼	c	sugar
3	T	lemon juice
⅓	c	slivered blanched almonds
½	tsp	ground nutmeg
¼	tsp	salt
¼	tsp	grated orange peel

In 8 to 10-quart kettle mix peaches and cantaloupe. Bring mixture to full rolling boil; stir constantly. Add sugar and lemon juice. Bring mixture again to full rolling boil. Boil, uncovered 12 minutes. Add the almonds, nutmeg, salt and orange peel. Boil hard, uncovered, till syrup sheets off metal spoon, 4 to 5 minutes. Remove from heat; quickly skim off foam with metal spoon. Pour at once into hot sterilized jars; seal.
Yield: 7 half-pint.

MIXED FRUIT CONSERVE

1½	lbs	peaches
1	lb	pears
¾	lb	red plums
4	c	sugar
1	c	raisins
½	c	chopped nuts
¼	c	lemon juice

Peel, pit and dice peaches; measure 3 cups. Peel, core and dice pears; measure 2 cups. Pit and dice plums; measure 2 cups. In an 8- to 10-quart kettle combine peaches, pears, plums, sugar, and raisins. Heat and stir till sugar dissolves. Bring fruit mixture to full rolling boil. Boil hard, uncovered, for 15 to 18 minutes or till syrup "sheets" from metal spoon, stirring constantly. Stir in nuts and lemon juice. Remove from heat. Skim off foam with metal spoon. Ladle at once into hot, clean, half-pint jars, leaving ¼-inch headspace. Wipe jar rims; adjust lids. Process in boiling water bath for 15 minutes.

Yield: 6 to 7 half-pints.

ALMOND-PEACH CONSERVE

1		unpeeled chopped orange
7	c	firm ripe peeled, chopped peaches
5	c	sugar
½	tsp	ground ginger
½	c	blanched, slivered almonds

Add orange to peaches; cook gently about 15 to 20 minutes. Add sugar and ginger. Bring slowly to boiling, stirring occasionally until sugar dissolves. Cook rapidly until thick, about 15 minutes. As mixture thickens, stir occasionally to prevent sticking. Add nuts the last 5 minutes of cooking. Pour, boiling hot, into hot jars, leaving ¼-inch headspace. Adjust lids and process 15 minutes in boiling water bath.

Yield: about 8 half-pints.

PEACH AND NECTARINE JAM

1½	lb	ripe peaches
1½	lb	ripe nectarines
1	pkg	(1¾ oz) powdered fruit pectin
2	T	lemon juice
3½	c	sugar
1	c	light corn syrup

Peel, pit and quarter peaches and nectarines. Finely chop and measure 1½ cups each. In 8-quart stainless steel or enamel saucepot stir together peaches, nectarines, pectin and lemon juice until well blended. Stirring constantly, bring to full rolling boil. Stir in sugar and corn syrup. Return to full rolling boil stirring constantly; boil rapidly 1 minute. Remove from heat; skim surface. Immediately ladle into clean hot jars leaving ¼ inch headspace. Adjust lids and process in boiling water bath 5 minutes.

Yield: 6 half-pints.

SPICED PEACH JAM

Spicy - but good!

5	c	sugar
4	c	peeled, crushed peaches
½	tsp	ground cloves
½	tsp	ground cinnamon
½	tsp	ground allspice
1	pkg	(1¾ oz) powdered fruit pectin
		Red food coloring, optional

Measure sugar and set aside. Put crushed peaches into large kettle; add spices and pectin to fruit. Place over high heat. Stir until mixture comes to a full rolling boil; at once stir in sugar. Bring back to full rolling boil (a boil that cannot be stirred down); boil for 1 minute, stirring constantly. Take from heat. Alternately stir and skim (to remove foam) for about 5 minutes. While stirring add a few drops of red food coloring to brighten color of jam, if desired. Pour into clean, hot, dry jars. Seal at once with self-sealing lids or cover at once with 1/8-inch layer of melted paraffin. Store in a cool, dry place.

Yield: 6 to 8 half-pints.

National Peach Council

SPARKLING PEACH MARMALADE

1	sm	orange
1		lemon
¼	c	water
3	lbs	peaches
1	pkg	(1¾ oz) powdered fruit pectin
5	c	sugar

Cut orange and lemon in quarters; remove seeds. Slice orange and lemon quarters crosswise in paper-thin slices. In medium saucepan combine fruit slices and water. Cover and simmer the orange-lemon mixture 20 minutes. Peel, pit and finely chop or grind peaches. In 8- to 10-quart kettle combine orange-lemon mixture and peaches. Stir pectin into fruit mixture. Bring mixture to full rolling boil; stir in sugar. Bring again to full rolling boil, stirring constantly. Boil hard, uncovered, 1 minute. Remove from heat; quickly skim off foam. Pour at once into hot sterilized jars; seal.

Yield: 7 to 8 half-pints.

ROSY PEACH-BANANA JAM

Impress your family with this creation!

3¼	c	peeled mashed peaches
1	c	mashed banana
½	c	coarsely chopped maraschino cherries
2	T	lemon juice
1	pkg	(1¾ oz) powdered fruit pectin
6	c	sugar

Combine peaches, banana, cherries, lemon juice and fruit pectin in a large saucepot; stir well. Place over high heat and bring to a boil, stirring frequently. Quickly stir in sugar; bring to a boil; boil 1 minute, stirring constantly. Remove from heat; skim off foam with a metal spoon. Quickly ladle jam into hot sterilized jars, leaving ¼-inch headspace; cover at once with metal lids, and screw metal bands tight. Process in boiling-water bath for 5 minutes.

Yield: 7 half-pints.

GLOWING PEACH-ORANGE MARMALADE

2	qts	peeled, chopped firm-ripe peaches
¾	c	sliced orange peel
1½	c	chopped orange pulp
2	T	lemon juice
5	c	sugar

Combine all ingredients; bring slowly to boiling, stirring occasionally until sugar dissolves. Cook rapidly until thick, about 30 minutes. As mixture thickens, stir frequently to prevent sticking. Remove from heat and skim off foam with a metal spoon. Pour, boiling hot, into hot sterilized jars leaving ¼ inch headspace. Adjust lids and process 10 to 15 minutes in boiling water bath.

Yield: about 8 half-pints.

PEACH-ORANGE MARMALADE WITH CHERRIES

So simple, but so good!

12		to 15 peaches
1	jar	(6 oz) maraschino cherries
1		orange
		Sugar

Cut peeled peaches in small pieces and grind cherries and orange (include rind). Mix together and for every cup of fruit mixture add an equal amount of sugar. Cook one hour. Spoon into hot jars and seal immediately.

Yield: 8 half-pints.

OLD FASHION PEACH JAM

2	qts	peeled, crushed peaches
½	c	water
6	c	sugar

Combine peaches and water, cook gently 10 minutes. Add sugar, slowly bring to boiling, stirring occasionally until sugar dissolves. Cook rapidly until thick, about 15 minutes, stirring frequently to prevent sticking. Pour, boiling hot into hot sterilized jars. Adjust lids and process 10-15 minutes.

Yield: about 4 pints.

SPICY PEACH-APRICOT JAM

2	lbs	peaches
1	lb	apricots
2	T	lemon juice
1	pkg	(1¾ oz) powdered fruit pectin
5½	c	sugar
1	tsp	ground cinnamon
½	tsp	ground allspice

Peel, pit and coarsely grind peaches and apricots. Place fruits in an 8 or 10-quart kettle. Add lemon juice and stir in pectin. Bring to a full rolling boil, stirring constantly. Stir in sugar and spices. Return to a full rolling boil. Boil hard, uncovered, for 1 minute, stirring constantly. Remove from heat; quickly skim off foam with a metal spoon. Ladle jam at once into hot, sterilized jars, leaving a ¼-inch headspace. Wipe jar rims, adjust lids and process in boiling water bath for 15 minutes.

Yield: 7 to 8 half-pints.

PEACH-ALMOND JAM

3	lbs	fresh peaches
½	c	chopped almonds
¼	c	lemon juice
7	c	sugar
1	pkg	(3 oz) liquid fruit pectin
¼	tsp	almond extract

Wash thoroughly; do not peel peaches. Cut into chunks, removing pits. Grind or chop very find in blender. Measure 4 cups peaches into a heavy 6- to 8-quart kettle. Stir in almonds, lemon juice and sugar. Put over high heat and stir until mixture comes to a full, rolling boil. Boil hard for 1 minute, stirring constantly. Remove from heat. At once, stir in fruit pectin and almond extract. Skim off foam with metal spoon, then stir and skim for 5 minutes to cool slightly and prevent floating fruit. Ladle into sterilized jars. Seal at once with self-sealing lids or cover with 1/8-inch melted paraffin.

Yield: 11 half-pints.

National Peach Council

PLUM AND PEACH JAM

1¼	lbs	peaches
¾	lb	fully ripe Italian prune plums
1	pkg	(1¾ oz) powdered fruit pectin
2	T	lemon juice
5½	c	sugar

Peel, pit and coarsely grind peaches; measure 2 cups ground peaches. Pit and finely chop fully ripe plums; measure 2 cups. In 8-to 10-quart kettle combine peaches, plums, pectin and lemon juice. Bring to full rolling boil (a boil that cannot be stirred down), stirring constantly. Stir in sugar. Return to full rolling boil. Boil hard, uncovered for 1 minute, stirring constantly. Remove from heat, quickly skim off foam with metal spoon. Ladle at once into hot, clean half-pint jars, leaving ¼ inch headspace. Wipe jar rims; adjust lids. Process in boiling water bath for 15 minutes.

Yield: about 6 half-pints.

RASPBERRY AND PEACH JAM

For a gift with a special homemade touch.

2	lbs	fully ripe peaches
1		10 oz pkg frozen red raspberries, thawed
¼	c	lemon juice
6	c	sugar
1		pouch (3 oz) liquid pectin

Peel, pit and crush fully ripe peaches. Measure thawed raspberries and add crushed peaches to make 4 cups. Combine fruit and lemon juice in very large saucepan. Stir sugar into fruit. Place over high heat, bring to a full rolling boil and boil hard 1 minute, stirring constantly. Remove from heat; at once stir in pectin. Skim off foam with metal spoon. Stir and skim 5 minutes to cool slightly and prevent floating fruit. Ladle quickly into jars. Cover at once with 1/8 inch hot paraffin.

Yield: about 10 half-pints.

God has two dwellings: one in heaven, and the other in meek and thankful hearts.

Izaak Walton

GINGERED PEACH JAM

6	c	sugar
4½	c	peeled, chopped or ground peaches
¼	c	finely slivered candied ginger
1	pkg	(1¾ oz) powdered fruit pectin

Measure sugar and set aside.

Measure peaches into a large saucepot; add ginger. Add fruit pectin to fruit and mix well. Place over high heat and stir until mixture comes to a hard boil; at once stir in sugar. Bring to a full rolling boil and boil hard 1 minute, stirring constantly. Remove from heat and skim off foam with metal spoon. Then stir and skim for 5 minutes to cool slightly and prevent floating fruit. Ladle quickly into sterilized jars. Cover at once with 1/8-inch layer of hot paraffin.

Yield: about 10 half-pints.

PEAR-PEACH JAM

Super special creation.

1	lb	pears
1	lb	peaches
2	T	lemon juice
1	pkg	(1¾ oz) powdered fruit pectin
5½	c	sugar

Peel, core and grind or finely chop pears; measure 2 cups. Peel, pit and grind or finely chop peaches; measure 2 cups. In 8 or 10-quart kettle combine pears, peaches, lemon juice and pectin. Bring mixture to full rolling boil. Stir in sugar, bring mixture again to full rolling boil. Boil hard, uncovered, 1 minute, stirring constantly. Remove from heat; quickly skim off foam with metal spoon. Pour at once into hot sterilized jars; seal.

Yield: 7 half-pints.

RADIANT PEACH JAM

4	c	peeled, ground peaches
1	pkg	(1¾ oz) powdered fruit pectin
2	T	lemon juice
5½	c	sugar

In 8- to 10-quart kettle combine peaches, pectin and lemon juice. Bring to full rolling boil (a boil that cannot be stirred down), stirring constantly. Stir in sugar. Return to full rolling boil. Boil hard, uncovered, for 1 minute, stirring constantly. Remove from heat, quickly skim off foam with metal spoon. Ladle at once into hot, clean half-pint jars, leaving ¼-inch headspace. Wipe jar rims; adjust lids. Process in boiling water bath for 15 minutes.

Yield: 6 to 7 half-pints.

CHERRY-PEACH JAM

Dazzling elegance.

1	lb	tart red cherries
1¼	lbs	peaches
2	T	lemon juice
1	pkg	(1¾ oz) powdered fruit pectin
4	c	sugar

Sort, wash and remove the stems from the cherries. Pit and coarsely chop the cherries; measure 1½ cups. Peel, pit and coarsely chop the peaches; measure 2 cups. In an 8- to 10-quart kettle combine the chopped fruit and lemon juice. Add the powdered fruit pectin to the mixture; mix well. Bring mixture to full rolling boil. Stir in sugar. Bring again to full rolling boil, stirring constantly. Boil hard, uncovered, 1 minute. Remove from heat; quickly skim off foam with metal spoon. Pour at once into hot sterilized jars; seal.

Yield: 5 half-pints.

It's the little things in life that count,
The things of every day;
Just the simple things that we can do,
The kind words we can say.

Virginia Katherine Oliver

PEACH CATSUP

3	qts	fresh pitted and sliced peaches
2	c	chopped onion
1	c	EACH white vinegar and sugar
2		whole cinnamon sticks
1	tsp	EACH whole cloves and allspice, tied in cheesecloth.

In large saucepot, combine all ingredients; bring to boil. Cook over medium-high heat 45 to 50 minutes, stirring occasionally until mixture thickens and fruit is tender. Remove and discard spices. Puree mixture in 2 batches in blender or food processor. Pour into hot sterilized jars; adjust lids and process in boiling water bath 15 minutes. Store in cool place.

Yield: about 4 half-pints.

California Tree Fruit Agreement

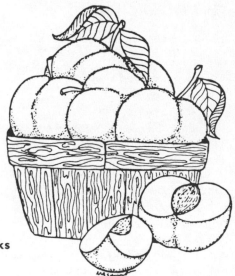

SPICY PICKLED PEACHES

6		4-inch cinnamon sticks
1	T	whole allspice
2	T	whole cloves
1		piece gingerroot
1	qt	cider vinegar
1	qt	water
¼	tsp	salt
8	c	sugar
6	lbs	medium-size firm peaches

Tie spices loosely in a cheesecloth bag and boil with vinegar, water, salt and sugar for 10 minutes. Add peeled whole peaches, a few at a time and simmer until tender. When all are done, remove spice bag. Pack peaches into hot sterilized jars and fill with boiling syrup; seal.

Yield: about 6 pints.

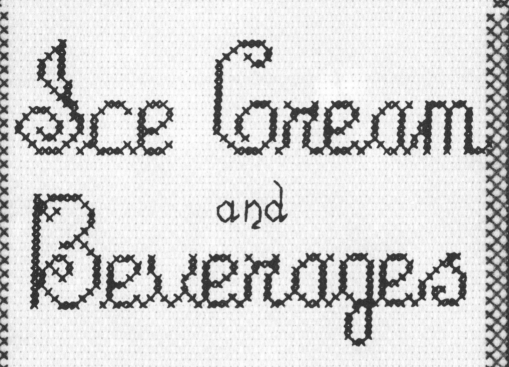

Ice Cream and Beverages

Ice cream and water ices crossed the Atlantic at the time of the early colonial settlements and have been enjoyed in homes in America ever since. An Ice, the oldest of the frozen refreshments is simply a frozen mixture of fruit juice or fruit puree and a sweetener mixed with water, especially delightful when that fruit is peaches! "Nothing ever tastes quite as good as homemade ice cream," or so some say, especially if it is peach homemade ice cream. All ice creams are not made in an ice cream freezer; many can be made in the freezer compartment of the refrigerator or home freezer. Sherbet is a very popular frozen refreshment that is made from a mixture of fruit or fruit juices, water and sweeteners, to which milk, beaten egg whites and gelatin are often added. On a hot summer day, who can resist ice cream, sherbet, or one of the many peach-flavored beverages?

PEACHY TWIRL COOLER

3	md	peaches
1	T	lemon juice
1	tsp	almond extract
2	T	sugar
1	c	milk
1	c	peach ice cream

Peel, pit, and slice peaches. Reserve 2 slices; dip in lemon juice. Place remainder of the sliced peaches in the blender and puree. Add lemon juice, almond extract, sugar and milk; cover and blend thoroughly. Mix in peach ice cream. Pour into large glasses; garnish each with reserved peach slice and a sprig of mint. Serve immediately.

Makes two 12-ounce servings.

National Peach Council

FRESH PEACH MELBA FLOAT

3		fresh peaches, peeled and sliced
1		banana, sliced
1	pt	raspberry sherbet
		ginger ale

Arrange peach and banana slices in 6 stemmed glasses. Top with a scoop of sherbet. Set glasses in freezer 15 minutes to frost. To serve, fill glasses with ginger ale; accompany with straw and spoon.

Yield: 6 drinks.

California Tree Fruit Agreement

DELECTABLE PEACH FROST

For a hot summer evening.

3	md	ripe peaches, pitted, peeled, quartered
½	c	light corn syrup
¼	tsp	ground ginger
1	c	lemon sherbet
½	c	ginger ale
2		scoops vanilla ice cream

In blender container place peaches, corn syrup and ginger; cover. Blend on medium speed 30 seconds or just until smooth. Add sherbet and ginger ale; cover. Blend on medium speed 15 seconds or just until smooth. Pour into 2 large glasses. Top each with ice cream.

Makes 2 servings.

COOL PEACH REFRESHER

¾	c	cold milk
½	c	chilled cut-up peaches, fresh or canned
¼	tsp	salt
2-3		drops almond extract
½	c	vanilla ice cream

Put all ingredients **except ice cream** into blender. Cover and process until smooth. Stop and add the ice cream; cover and process 3 to 5 seconds longer.

Yield: 2 - 6 oz servings.

South Carolina Peach Council

PEACHY ICE CREAM SODAS

Hospitality in a hurry.

2	c	sugar
1	c	water
2	c	fresh peeled and finely chopped peaches
		Juice of 1 lemon
½	tsp	almond extract
1	qt	vanilla ice cream
8		tall soda glasses
		Sparkling water

In saucepan, mix sugar and water. Stir until sugar is dissolved; then boil. Remove from heat; cool. Add peaches, lemon juice and almond extract. Cover and refrigerate. To serve: spoon a little peach syrup into each soda glass. Drop in a scoop of ice cream. Top with more syrup. Fill glass with sparkling water. Top with another scoop of ice cream. Serve with straws and long-handled spoons.

Makes 8 servings.

California Tree Fruit Agreement

MALTED PEACH REFRESHER

1		fresh peach, sliced
1		egg
1		scoop vanilla ice cream
½	T	instant malted milk

In blender container, blend all ingredients. Pour into tall glass. Serve with spoon and straw. For shake, leave out the malt and add ¼ teaspoon almond or vanilla extract.

Makes one 8-ounce serving.

California Tree Fruit Agreement

A PEACH COOLER

1	T	thawed lemonade or limeade concentrate
1	pt	vanilla ice cream
2		peeled and sliced peaches

Combine concentrate and ice cream in blender. Blend until smooth. Add peaches and blend just for a second. Pour into glasses and place in freezer until slushy. "Drink" with a spoon. A dash of dried mint - added to the juice and ice cream - gives a zip to the flavor.

SAVORY PEACH SLUSH

1	c	sugar
½	c	light corn syrup
2	c	water, divided
1	can	(29 oz) peaches, drained
¼	c	lemon juice

Combine sugar, corn syrup and **1 cup** water in a small saucepan. Bring mixture to a boil, stirring constantly until sugar dissolves; reduce heat, and simmer 3 minutes. Cool. Place peaches in container of food processor or electric blender; process until smooth. Add remaining **1 cup** of water; process until thoroughly combined. Combine cooled syrup, peach mixture and lemon juice; stir well. Pour into an 8-inch square pan; freeze. Stir a few times during freezing process. Let stand at room temperature 10 minutes before serving.

Yield: about 6½ cups.

GOLDEN GOODIE

For each peach, peeled and sliced, add ⅓ cup orange juice in the electric blender and blend.

South Carolina Peach Council

MELODY PEACH PUNCH

A refreshing fruit combination!

2	c	sugar
2	c	water
1	pt	homemade peach nectar*, thawed, if frozen
1	can	(6 oz) frozen orange juice concentrate, thawed
1	can	(6 oz) frozen pineapple juice concentrate, thawed
¾	c	lemon juice
2	lg	bottles gingerale, chilled

Combine sugar and water. Stir to dissolve. Add all juices. Chill. Just before serving, add gingerale. (May be topped with lemon or lime sherbet.)
Makes 20-25 servings.

*Homemade Peach Nectar: peel, remove seed, cut in quarters and sprinkle peaches with color keeper. Place peach quarters in food blender and convert to liquid (15 to 30 seconds). Pour the puree into pint freezer containers. Stir in 2 tablespoons sugar per pint. Leave ½-inch headspace for expansion; cover air tight and freeze.
Suggested uses:
1. Thaw slightly and eat as peach ice.
2. Thaw completely and serve as a drink.
3. Thaw and use in making ice cream.
4. Thaw, dilute with equal amount of water and serve as a drink.
5. Pep Shake - Add 1 egg and ½ cup vanilla ice cream to 1 cup thawed peach nectar in food blender. Turn on low speed, blend until ice cream is soft.

S.C. Department of Agriculture

PEACH ICE

8		peaches, peeled and quartered
1	c	sugar
¼	c	lemon juice
2	c	ginger ale

Put peaches, sugar and lemon juice into blender container. Blend until smooth. Stir in ginger ale. Pour into ice cube trays and freeze until mushy.
Yield: about 5 cups.

California Tree Fruit Agreement

ORANGE PEACH SHAKE

1	can	(7½ oz) sliced peaches
2	c	orange juice
2	T	peach yogurt
1	pt	vanilla ice cream,
		softened and cut into pieces
2	T	milk

Drain peaches, reserving 2 tablespoons syrup. Combine peaches, 2 tablespoons reserved syrup and remaining ingredients in the container of electric blender; process until smooth.

Yield: about 5 cups.

FRUIT BOWL FLIP

A tempting array of fruits blended into a delightful treat.

4-5		fresh peaches, sliced
½	pt	strawberries, stemmed
2	c	cubed pineapple (fresh or canned)
1	pt	plain yogurt
		Honey to taste

Combine and chill prepared fruits. For each drink; measure 1 cup of fruit into blender. Add ¼ cup yogurt and honey to taste. Blend until smooth. Pour into glasses; serve at once.

Makes 8 (8 oz) drinks.

California Tree Fruit Agreement

PINEAPPLE-PEACH SHAKE

1	pt	vanilla ice cream
¾	c	peeled and sliced peaches, chilled
¾	c	unsweetened pineapple juice, chilled

Combine all ingredients in blender or shaker; blend until smooth. Pour into chilled glasses.

Makes 4 servings.

Happiness is homemade peach ice cream!
Select from a tempting variety of melt-in-your mouth peach ice cream.

SOUTHERN PEACH ICE CREAM

2	qts	fresh peach puree
		Juice of 2 lemons
1	tsp	almond flavoring
1	pt	whipping cream, not whipped
2½	c	sugar (approximately)

Select ripe peaches, wash well, peel if desired, but not necessary, pit and puree. Mix all ingredients, being sure sugar is dissolved. Pour into the freezing can of the ice cream freezer and freeze according to the manufacturer's instructions.

S.C. Department of Agriculture

DELUXE PEACH ICE CREAM

6	c	mashed peaches
3	c	sugar
5		eggs
¼	tsp	salt
1	tsp	vanilla extract
1	c	whipping cream, whipped
1	c	half-and-half
1	qt	whole milk

Combine peaches and **1 cup** sugar; stir well, and set aside. Beat eggs with electric mixer at medium speed until frothy. Gradually add **2 cups** sugar, beating until thick. Add salt, vanilla and ½ **cup** milk; beat until sugar is dissolved. Stir in **whipped** cream, half-and-half and peaches. Pour mixture into freezer can of 1-gallon hand-turned or electric freezer. Add enough milk to fill can two-thirds full. Freeze according to manufacturer's instructions. Let ripen at least 1 hour.

Do not pray for easy lives, pray to be stronger! Do not pray for tasks equal to your powers, pray for powers equal to your tasks.

Phillips Brooks

GEORGIA PEACH ICE CREAM

1¾	c	sugar
4	c	mashed peaches
4		eggs, well beaten
1	can	sweetened condensed milk
1	T	vanilla flavoring
2	qts	whole milk
		Few drops of red food coloring, if desired.

Mix ¾ **cup** sugar with mashed peaches. Combine well beaten eggs with **1 cup** sugar, condensed milk and vanilla flavoring. Add peach/sugar mixture to egg mixture; add whole milk and freeze according to manufacturer's instructions.

Georgia Peach Commission

FAVORITE PEACH ICE CREAM

2	lbs	fully ripe peaches
¾	c	sugar
1	T	lemon juice
2		eggs
3	c	whole milk
1	c	whipping cream
2/3	c	light corn syrup
1	tsp	vanilla

Peel, pit and finely chop peaches. Stir in ¼ **cup** of the sugar and lemon juice; set aside. In large bowl with mixer at medium speed beat eggs until light and frothy. Gradually add remaining ½ **cup** of sugar, beating until dissolved. Add milk, cream, corn syrup and vanilla, beating until blended. Stir in peach mixture. Freeze in 4-quart ice cream freezer following manufacturer's directions.

REALLY GOOD PEACH ICE CREAM

4	c	whipping cream
1	c	whole milk
4		eggs
½	c	sweetened condensed milk
2½	c	sugar
¼	tsp	salt
2	qts	fresh peaches, mashed; measure juice
1	pt	peach juice

Combine **2 cups** cream with milk in top of a double boiler. Place over boiling water and cook until scalded. Beat eggs slightly and add sweetened condensed milk, sugar and salt. Blend in small amount of cream mixture to egg mixture slowly. Stir back into cream mixture and cook for 5 minutes longer or until mixture coats a spoon, stirring constantly. Stir in peaches, peach juice and remaining **2 cups** cream. Freeze in an ice cream freezer according to freezer directions.

SUNDAY PEACH ICE CREAM

8		peaches, very ripe and unpeeled
1	tsp	almond flavoring
		Dash freshly squeezed lemon juice
		Sugar
1	pt	whipping cream

Mash peaches, including skins and juices, with a fork or use a blender. Add almond flavoring and lemon juice. Add sugar to taste. Whip cream and blend thoroughly with peach mixture. Pour in ice tray and freeze. Remove from tray and cut into squares.

Makes 6 servings.

PEACH CUSTARD ICE CREAM

2		eggs, beaten
1½	c	whole milk
1	c	sugar
1/8	tsp	salt
1	tsp	vanilla extract
1½	c	whipping cream
1½	c	peach puree (3 or 4 peaches)

Combine eggs, milk, sugar and salt in saucepan. Cook over low heat, stirring constantly, until mixture coats metal spoon lightly. DO NOT BOIL. Remove from heat; stir in vanilla and cream. Cool. Peel and pit peaches, then puree to make 1½ cups. Add to custard mixture. Pour into 2-quart ice cream freezer and freeze according to manufacturer's directions.

California Tree Fruit Agreement

PEACH CUSTARD ICE CREAM

1	qt	whole milk
1	c	cream or evaporated milk
3		eggs
1	c	sugar
1	T	all-purpose flour
1/8	tsp	salt
2	qts	mashed peaches
1	T	vanilla

Scald milk and cream. Beat eggs and combine with half of the sugar. Mix flour and salt with remainder of sugar. Blend all with hot milk and cream. Cook until it thickens. Add mashed peaches, vanilla and freeze according to manufacturer's instructions.

Georgia Peach Commission

QUICK PEACH ICE CREAM

4		to 6 peaches (1½ cups puree)
1	T	lemon juice
1	c	whipping cream
1	c	powdered sugar

Peel peaches and remove pits. Put peaches and lemon juice into blender. Cover, blend and puree until smooth. Whip cream until it holds a soft peak. Add powdered sugar and continue to beat until stiff. Fold in 1½ cups peach puree. Pour into refrigerator tray and freeze for 2 to 4 hours or until firm.

Makes 4 to 6 servings.

YUMMY PEACH SHERBET

1	env	(1 T) unflavored gelatin
1	c	sugar
		Dash salt
½	c	water
2	c	fresh peach puree
1	can	(13 oz) evaporated milk
2		egg whites

In large saucepan combine gelatin, ½ to ¾ **cup** sugar and salt. Stir in water; heat and stir till gelatin dissolves. Stir in peach puree and evaporated milk. Turn into a 9x9x2-inch pan; cover and freeze till firm. In small mixer bowl beat egg whites till **soft** peaks form; gradually add ¼ **cup** sugar beating till **stiff** peaks form. Break frozen mixture into chunks; turn into chilled large mixer bowl. Beat till fluffy. Fold in egg whites. Return to pan; cover and freeze till firm.

PEACH SHERBET

¾	c	peach puree
¼	c	sugar
¾	c	orange juice
2	T	lemon juice

Combine peach puree with sugar, orange juice and lemon juice. Pour into a 1-quart freezer tray and freeze until mushy, stirring occasionally. Turn into a bowl and beat until smooth with an electric or rotary mixer. Return to tray and freeze until firm, stirring once or twice. Recipe may be doubled.

Yield: 1 pint.

Georgia Peach Commission

HOT WEATHER PEACH SHERBET

2/3	c	sweetened condensed milk
2	T	lemon juice
2	T	melted butter
½	c	water
1	c	crushed fresh peaches
2		egg whites, stiffly beaten

Blend the milk with the lemon juice, butter and water in a bowl. Add the peaches and chill. Fold in egg whites and pour into freezing tray. Freeze until partially frozen, then remove to a bowl. Beat until smooth and pour back into freezing tray. Freeze until firm.

Makes 6 servings.

SPECIAL PEACH SHERBET
(may be prepared ahead of time)

1½	c	sugar
½	c	water
3	c	fresh peaches
		Juice of 2 oranges
1	tsp	freshly squeezed lemon juice
2		egg whites, beat until stiff
1	c	whipping cream, whipped

Cook sugar and water together until syrup spins a thread. Let cool. Peel peaches and partially mash them; they should not be pureed. Combine with the cooked syrup, add lemon and orange juice and blend well. Turn into freezer tray and freeze until not quite firm. Remove to large bowl, beat well and fold in egg whites, then whipped cream. Return to freezer to harden. Stir several times during freezing.

Makes 8 servings.

Every life we touch is a field, everything we do and all the words we speak, are seed. What will the harvest be?

Rowland

CALIFORNIA PEACH ICE CREAM

1	env	(1 T) unflavored gelatin
½	c	whole milk, cold
½	c	whole milk, heated to boiling
3	c	chopped unpeeled fresh peaches
¾	c	sugar
¼	tsp	vanilla extract
2	c	whipping cream, whipped

In 5-cup blender, sprinkle gelatin over **cold** milk; let stand 3 to 4 minutes. Add **hot** milk and process at low speed until gelatin is completely dissolved, about 2 minutes. Gradually add peaches (unpeeled peaches should be washed), sugar and vanilla and process at high speed until smooth. Pour into bowl and chill, stirring occasionally, until mixture mounds slightly when dropped from spoon. Fold gelatin mixture into whipped cream. Pour into 2 freezer trays or 8-inch baking pan, freeze until firm.

Misc.

Enter the world of gourmet delights with these out-of-the-ordinary recipes that offer many varied and innovative ways to use peaches from entrees to snack suggestions. There is a potpourri of taste-tempting and inviting main dishes and side dishes with a difference, extremely good fruit casseroles, spectacular breakfast and brunch ideas, festive dessert crepes, party fondue, dressed-up vegetables and even soup using the bounty of the harvest—peaches!

The omelet is ideal for a planned brunch or Sunday supper, but it is a real winner to serve unexpected drop-in visitors. The delicious smell while the omelet cooks, will make anyone hungry.

PEACH OMELET

1	c	sliced peaches
		Color keeper
4		slices bacon
6	lg	eggs
2	T	water
1	tsp	fresh or freeze-dried chopped chives
¼	tsp	salt
1/8	tsp	pepper
		Paprika, if desired

Mix peaches with color keeper to prevent browning; set aside at room temperature. Using 10-inch skillet, fry bacon until crisp and drain. Remove all but 2 tablespoons bacon grease from skillet. Beat eggs in bowl until foamy; add water. Crumble bacon and mix into eggs along with chives, salt and pepper. Heat reserved bacon grease until it just begins to sizzle. Add egg mixture; arrange well-drained peach slices over top. Cook over medium heat until mixture begins to set around edges; with a spatula gently lift edges as they set; tilting skillet to allow uncooked egg mixture to run under omelet. Cook until all egg mixture is set and hot throughout but still moist on surface. Add paprika, if desired. Cut in wedges and serve at once.

Makes 3 to 4 servings.

National Peach Council

DESSERT CREPES WITH FRESH PEACH FILLING

Dessert Crepes

2		eggs
¾	c	flour
2	T	sugar
1	c	whole milk
½	tsp	vanilla extract
½	tsp	almond extract
1	T	butter, melted and cooled

Beat eggs and add flour and sugar; mix well. (If too thick add a little of the milk.) Add milk, flavorings and melted butter; mix well. Set aside and let stand for at least an hour. To cook crepes heat a 5-inch crepe pan or small frying pan until a small amount of butter bubbles. Pour 1½ tablespoons of crepe batter in pan tilting pan rapidly until the bottom is covered. Cook crepe on one side for about 1½ minutes or until lightly brown. Turn crepe and cook for about a minute on the other side. Turn crepe out onto a paper towel. If you will not be using immediately, stack crepes with wax paper between each crepe.

Yield: about 20 crepes.

Fresh Peach Filling

3	c	fresh peach puree
2	tsp	ascorbic acid
3	T	cornstarch
1	c	brown sugar
1/8	tsp	salt
3	T	butter
¼	tsp	almond flavoring
2	c	diced fresh peaches

Mix peach puree, ascorbic acid, cornstarch, brown sugar, and salt together in sauce pan. Place over medium heat and cook until thick, stirring constantly. Add butter and mix until melted. Add flavoring and diced peaches. Use as filling for Dessert Crepes. If desired, each crepe can be topped with a dollop of sour cream or sweetened whipped cream.

Yield: 20 crepes using ¼ cup of filling for each crepe.

National Peach Council

PANCAKES WITH FRUIT TOPPING

Fruit Topping: Drain 1 can (16 oz) sliced peaches, reserving ¼ cup syrup. Combine peaches, reserved syrup, ½ cup apricot preserves, ⅓ cup maraschino cherries, cut in half, ¼ cup butter, 2 teaspoons lemon juice and ½ tsp vanilla extract in a medium saucepan. Bring mixture to a boil, stirring occasionally; reduce heat and add 3 medium bananas, cut into ¼-inch slices. Simmer until bananas are heated through. Keep warm for serving.

Yield: 3¾ cups topping

2	c	biscuit mix
1		egg
1⅓	c	whole milk
1	c	100% natural cereal, crushed

Combine biscuit mix, egg and milk; beat until smooth. Stir in cereal. For each pancake, pour about ¼ cup batter onto a lightly greased hot griddle or skillet. When pancakes have a bubbly surface and slightly dry edges, turn to cook other side. Serve with Fruit Topping.

Yield: 14 pancakes

There is no such thing as bad weather; the good Lord simply sends us different kinds of good weather.

John Ruskin

CHEESE BLINTZES

Blintze - a thin rolled pancake with a filling usually of cream cheese.

2	pkg	(3 oz ea) cream cheese, softened
1	ctn	(12 oz) dry curd cottage cheese
1		egg, beaten
2	T	sugar
1	tsp	grated lemon rind
		Crepes*
3	T	butter or margarine, divided
		Commercial sour cream
		Peach preserves
		Fresh peaches, optional

Combine cream and cheese and cottage cheese; beat until smooth. Stir in egg, sugar and lemon rind; chill 15 to 20 minutes. Spoon about 3 tablespoons cheese filling in center of each crepe. Fold right and left sides over filling; then fold bottom and top over filling, forming a square. Melt 2 tablespoons butter in a large skillet. Place half of blintzes in skillet, seam side down. Cook over medium heat until lightly browned, turning once; remove from skillet and keep warm. Melt remaining tablespoon butter in skillet; repeat procedure with the remaining blintzes. Serve with sour cream and peach preserves. Garnish with fresh peaches, if desired.

Yield: 12 servings

*Crepes: Combine 1 cup all-purpose flour, ½ teaspoon salt and 1¼ cups whole milk, beating until smooth. Add 2 eggs and beat well; stir in 2 tablespoons melted butter. Refrigerate batter 1 hour. Brush the bottom of a 6- or 7-inch crepe pan or heavy skillet with vegetable oil; place pan over medium heat until just hot, not smoking. Pour 2 tablespoons batter into pan; quickly tilt pan in all directions so batter covers the pan with a thin film. Cook about 1 minute. Place crepes on a towel and allow to cool. Stack the crepes between layers of waxed paper to prevent sticking.

Yield: 12 crepes.

FANTASTIC PEACH FONDUE

1	can	(16 oz) peach halves (juice pack)
1	tsp	cornstarch
¼	tsp	ground cinnamon
1/8	tsp	ground allspice
½	tsp	vanilla
		Assorted fruits - apples, bananas, strawberries, etc.

In blender container combine undrained peaches, cornstarch, cinnamon and allspice. Cover, blend till nearly smooth. Pour into saucepan; cook and stir till thickened. Stir in vanilla. Transfer to fondue pot, keep warm over fondue burner. Serve with fruit on dippers.

HOLIDAY MORNING PEACH COFFEE CAKE
375° — 35-40 Minutes

Peach Filling:

½	c	sugar
3	T	cornstarch
¼	tsp	salt
1		egg yolk
¾	c	water
2	c	sliced peaches
1	tsp	ascorbic acid powder or lemon juice

Mix sugar, cornstarch and salt together in saucepan. Stir in egg yolk along with water, peaches and ascorbic acid or lemon juice. Cook over medium heat, stirring constantly until mixture comes to a boil. Set aside to cool.

Bread portion:

4	c	All-Purpose flour (approx.)
1	tsp	sugar
1	pkg	dry yeast
½	c	EACH milk and water
1	c	margarine
4		egg yolks

In a large bowl, mix **1¼ cups** flour with sugar and undissolved dry yeast. Combine milk, water and margarine in saucepan. Heat over low heat until liquids are very warm (120°-130°). Margarine does not need to melt. Gradually add to dry ingredients and beat 2 minutes at medium speed. Add 4 egg yolks and ½ cup flour. Beat 2 more minutes at high speed. Stir in **2-2½ cups** additional flour to make a soft moist dough. Divide dough in half. Place one-half in the bottom of 15x10x1-inch ungreased jelly roll pan. Spread with cooled peach filling. Roll remaining dough large enough to cover filling. Pinch edges together. Snip the surface of dough with scissors to let steam escape. Cover with towel and let rise in warm place for about 1 hour. Bake at 375° for 35-40 minutes or until done. Cool in pan and ice with peach glaze: mix 2 cups powdered sugar and 3 tablespoons peach puree, a tablespoon at a time, with a fork until desired consistency.

Makes 12 - 15 servings.

Georgia Peach Commission

A happy family is but an earlier heaven.

Bowring

PEACHY CAKE ROLL   375° — 12-15 Minutes

1	c	MINUS 2 T all-purpose flour
1	tsp	baking powder
¼	tsp	salt
3		eggs
1	c	sugar
⅓	c	water
1	tsp	vanilla
		Powdered sugar
		Peach filling*

Mix together flour, baking powder and salt. In another bowl, beat eggs about 5 minutes or until thick and lemon-colored. Gradually beat in sugar. On low speed, gradually blend in water and vanilla. Gradually add dry ingredients beating just until batter is smooth. Line a 15x10x1-inch jelly roll pan with waxed paper, then lightly grease the paper. Pour batter into pan and spread evenly. Bake at 375° for 12-15 minutes or until toothpick inserted in center comes out clean. Remove cake from oven and loosen edges. Invert pan onto a clean towel that has been dusted heavily with powdered sugar. Remove waxed paper. While cake is still hot, roll the cake and towel together from the narrow end. Cool on wire rack. When cool unroll cake and spread with Peach Filling*. Carefully roll cake again and sprinkle outside with powdered sugar. Cover and chill thoroughly before serving.

Peach Filling: Beat 8 ounces of cream cheese, softened, until smooth and fluffy. Add ½ cup powdered sugar and 1/8 teaspoon almond flavoring and beat till smooth. Mix in 1 cup finely diced peaches.

Makes 8 to 10 servings.

Georgia Peach Commission

PEACH AND HONEY BOATS

¼	c	butter
2	T	honey
2	T	sunflower seeds
4		slices wheat or sourdough bread
4		fresh peeled and sliced peaches

Combine butter, honey and sunflower seeds in a small mixing bowl. Spread on plain or toasted bread slices and top with peach slices.

Makes 4 open-faced sandwiches.

California Tree Fruit Agreement

DOUBLE DELIGHT PEACH PANCAKES

Peach Sauce: Melt 2 tablespoons butter and stir in 2 tablespoons flour. Mix ¼ cup sugar and 1 tablespoon cornstarch and add to butter/flour mixture, stirring until blended. Gradualty add 3 cups orange juice. Cook, stirring constantly over low heat until sauce bubbles and thickens. Fold in 3 fresh peaches, peeled and sliced and ¼ cup finely chopped maraschino cherries, optional. Reheat and simmer 5 minutes. Keep warm for serving.

1½	c	whole milk
3		eggs
6	T	butter or margarine, melted
3	c	sifted flour
2	T	baking powder
¼	c	sugar
1	tsp	salt
3		fresh peaches, peeled and diced

Combine milk, eggs and butter. Mix flour, baking powder, sugar and salt. Stir liquid ingredients into flour mixture until blended. Fold diced peaches into pancake batter. Pour batter by ⅓ cupful onto hot greased griddle. Cook until pancakes are golden underneath. Turn and brown on other side. Serve pancakes with Peach Sauce.

Makes 6 servings.

California Tree Fruit Agreement

LOAFER'S PEACHY FRENCH TOAST   425° — 25-30 Minutes

1	lb	Monterey Jack cheese OR other mild flavored cheese
8		slices white bread
4		eggs
1	c	half-and-half cream
½	tsp	salt
1/8	tsp	pepper
4½	c	fresh sliced peaches, sweetened to taste
		Powdered sugar

Cut cheese in ¼-inch thick slices. In well-buttered 9x5x3-inch glass loaf dish, arrange a layer of bread slices. Top with a layer of cheese. Repeat layers, ending with bread. Beat eggs; stir in half-and-half, salt and pepper. Pour over cheese and bread. Bake at 425° for 25 to 30 minutes or until puffy and golden brown. Cool in dish 10 to 15 minutes. Loosen edges; invert onto serving platter; surround with sliced peaches. Sprinkle with powdered sugar. Slice and serve.

Makes 6 servings.

California Tree Fruit Agreement

STUFFED FRENCH TOAST

1	pkg	(8 oz) cream cheese, softened
1½	tsp	vanilla
½	c	chopped walnuts
1		loaf (16 oz) French bread
4		eggs
1	c	whipping cream
½	tsp	ground nutmeg
1	jar	(12 oz) peach preserves
½	c	orange juice

Beat together the cream cheese and 1 teaspoon vanilla till fluffy. Stir in nuts; set aside. Cut bread into ten to twelve 1½-inch slices; cut a pocket in the top of each. Fill each with 1½ tablespoons of the cheese mixture. Beat together eggs, whipping cream, the remaining ½ teaspoon vanilla and the nutmeg. Using tongs, dip the filled bread slices in egg mixture, being careful not to squeeze out the filling. Cook on a lightly greased griddle till both sides are golden brown. To keep cooked slices hot for serving, place them on a baking sheet in a warm oven. Meanwhile, heat together the preserves and juice. To serve, drizzle the peach mixture over the hot French toast.

Yield: 10 to 12 stuffed slices.

Toppings for pancakes, waffles or French toast -

BLUEBERRY-PEACH PANCAKE SAUCE

1	c	fresh sliced peaches
1	c	fresh blueberries
2	T	sugar
½	c	apple juice
		Dash of ground nutmeg

Combine ½ **cup** peaches, ½ **cup** blueberries and remaining ingredients in a small saucepan. Bring to a boil; then reduce heat and simmer, uncovered, 15 minutes. Add remaining fruit, stirring well. Serve warm over pancakes, waffles or French toast.

Yield: 1½ cups.

PEACH TOPPING

2	c	peeled sliced peaches
2	T	lemon juice
¾	c	light corn syrup
2	T	corn oil margarine

In small bowl toss together peaches and lemon juice. In 2-quart saucepan stir together corn syrup and margarine. Stirring occasionally, bring to boil over medium heat and boil 5 minutes. Add peaches; reduce heat and simmer 5 minutes. Serve over pancakes, waffles or French toast.

Yield: about 2 cups.

Georgia Peach Commission

DELIGHTFUL TIMBALES WITH PEACH CREAM FILLING

Timbale irons are available at most kitchen shops or department stores. You can make the shells up to a week in advance and store in air-tight containers. When its party time, just add the filling.

Timbale Shells
1	c	all-purpose flour
1	c	milk
1		egg
1	T	sugar
½	tsp	vanilla
¼	tsp	salt
		Vegetable Oil

Combine flour, milk, egg, sugar, vanilla and salt. Beat at low speed of an electric mixer until smooth. Cover and chill 30 minutes or over-night. In a medium saucepan heat 2 to 3 inches of vegetable oil to 370°. Heat timbale iron in hot oil 1 minute. Drain excess oil from iron; dip into batter (do not coat top of iron with batter). Immediately return iron to hot oil. Cook about 30 seconds or until timbale is crisp and brown; lift iron slowly up and down to release. (Push timbale gently with a fork, if necessary.) Drain upside down on paper towels. Reheat iron 1 minute, and repeat procedure for each shell, stirring batter occasionally.

Yield: 2 dozen shells.

Filling
1	pkg	(3¾ oz) instant vanilla pudding mix
1½	c	whole milk
¼	tsp	almond extract
½	c	whipping cream, whipped
¾	c	canned, diced peaches, chilled

Prepare pudding mix according to package directions, using 1½ cups milk. Fold in almond extract, whipped cream and diced peaches. Spoon into Timbale Shells.

Yield: 2½ cups filling.

For that grand finale to a meal, serve dessert crepes. Made in advance, crepes can be quickly assembled when guests drop by. Some important tips to remember: it is important that the batter stand for one hour at room temperature or in the refrigerator for longer periods. (Batter may be stored in the refrigerator overnight; just stir before using.) After cook-ing, crepes should be turned out on paper towels, then stacked on a flat surface between waxed paper. At serving time, spoon the filling onto the side of the crepe that's least attractive so the prettiest side is showing. Ex-cess crepes should be stored between 2 paper plates and wrapped tightly. Store in refrigerator for several days or freeze for several months.

LEMON CREPES WITH FRUIT FILLING

2	c	frozen blueberries, thawed
⅓	c	granulated sugar
2½	c	cream-style cottage cheese, drained
1	c	sifted powdered sugar
1½	tsp	vanilla extract
		Lemon crepes*
1½	c	whipping cream
⅓	c	powdered sugar
2	c	canned, sliced peaches, drained

Combine blueberries and granulated sugar; stir gently and set aside. Combine cottage cheese, powdered sugar and vanilla extract in container of electric blender; process until mixture is smooth. Fill each crepe with about 2 tablespoons cottage cheese mixture and 1 tablespoon blueberries. Roll up and place seam side up on serving dish. Beat whipping cream until foamy; gradually add powdered sugar, beating until soft peaks form. Top each crepe with a dollop of whipped cream; garnish with peach slices and remaining blueberries.
Makes 16 servings.

*Lemon Crepes

¼	c	margarine, melted
½	c	cold water
¼	c	plus 2 T whole milk
2		whole eggs, plus 2 egg yolks
¾	c	all-purpose flour
1	T	sugar
¼	tsp	salt
1	tsp	grated lemon rind
¼	tsp	lemon extract
		Vegetable oil

Combine all ingredients except vegetable oil in container of electric blender; process 1 minute. Scrape down sides of the blender container with rubber spatula; process an additional 15 seconds. Refrigerate batter 1 hour. Brush the bottom of a 6-inch crepe pan with oil; place pan over medium heat until oil is just hot, not smoking. Pour 2 tablespoons batter into pan; quickly tilt pan in all directions so batter covers the pan in a thin film. Cook about 1 min. Lift edge of crepe to test for doneness. Crepe is ready for flipping when it can be shaken loose from pan. Flip crepe and cook about 30 seconds on other side. (This side is rarely more than spotty brown.) Place on a towel to cool. Stack crepes between layers of waxed papers to prevent sticking.
Yield: 16 crepes.

PEACH AND RICE DRESSING

A tasty accompaniment for fish and poultry!

4	lg	stalks celery
1	md	onion
4	T	margarine or butter
½	c	orange juice
¼	c	lemon juice
1	tsp	salt
½	tsp	thyme
¼	tsp	pepper
3	c	COOKED rice
4	md	peaches
		Water, if needed

Chop celery and onion and cook in margarine or butter until tender. Add juices, salt, thyme and pepper. Bring to a boil and stir in rice. Remove from heat, cover and let stand 5 minutes. Peel, pit and coarsely dice peaches; stir into rice mixture. If mixture is too dry, add a little water. Use to stuff poultry (allow 1 cup per pound); fish (allow ½ cup per pound); or bake in a casserole.

Yield: about 6 to 7 cups dressing.

National Peach Council

CANNED PEACH FRITTERS

Good served with baked or broiled ham!

1	can	(29 oz) sliced peaches
1	c	all-purpose flour, sifted before measuring
½	tsp	salt
1	tsp	baking powder
2		eggs, beaten
1	T	melted shortening
½	c	whole milk
		Vegetable oil

Drain peaches and sprinkle lightly with flour. Sift flour with salt and baking powder. Add well-beaten eggs, melted shortening and milk. Mix well. With a long-handled fork, dip fruit into batter. Allow excess batter to drain off. Lower fruit into hot shortening (375°) and fry 2-3 minutes or until a delicate brown. Drain on absorbent paper. Sprinkle with powdered sugar.
   Makes 4 to 5 servings.

South Carolina Peach Council

BEIGNETS DE PECHES

For that extra "something" to complete your meal!

		Vegetable oil
6	lg	fresh peeled, pitted and halved peaches
		Sugar to taste
1½	c	buttermilk pancake mix
1	c	water
		Powdered sugar

Place 1½ inches of vegetable oil in skillet and heat to 380°. Place peaches in bowl, sprinkle with sugar. Let stand 30 minutes. Blend pancake mix and water, beat just until smooth. Dip peaches into batter, covering completely. Fry in oil 2 to 3 minutes on each side. Drain on absorbent paper. Serve hot, sprinkled with powdered sugar.
   Makes 6 servings.

California Tree Fruit Agreement

PEACHES SUPREME   350° — 15-20 Minutes

Peaches Supreme goes well with chicken and turkey!

8		peach halves
2	T	melted butter
½	c	prepared mincemeat
		Sour Cream

Arrange the peach halves in a buttered baking dish and brush with melted butter. Place 1 teaspoon mincemeat in each half and spoon remaining mincemeat around peach halves. Bake at 350° for 15 to 20 minutes or until peaches are lightly browned and top with sour cream.
Makes 8 servings.

FLAMING PEACHES

Excitement plus!

Sprinkle brown sugar in hollows of peach halves in baking dish. Dot with butter. Broil slowly until sugar crusts. Put in center of each peach half a lump of sugar that has been soaked for 20 minutes in lemon extract. Light lump and bring to table flaming.

PLUM AND PEACH KABOBS   Broil — 3-5 Minutes

¼	c	butter or margarine
2	T	honey
1	T	lime juice
4	lg	bananas, peeled & cut
4		peaches, pitted and quartered
4	lg	plums, pitted and quartered

Combine butter, honey and lime juice. Cook over low heat, stirring occasionally, for 5 minutes. Arrange fruits alternately on skewers. Brush or roll in honey mixture. Broil 3 to 4 inches from heat for 3 to 5 minutes. Turn and brush fruit with mixture while broiling.

S.C. Department of Agriculture

EXOTIC PEACH HALVES

This is a quick and easy extra!

¼	tsp	ground ginger
¼	tsp	shredded lemon
1	T	dark brown sugar, firmly packed
4		canned peach halves, well drained

Combine ginger, lemon bits and brown sugar. Place peach halves in a 1-quart baking dish and sprinkle dry ingredients over the top. Place baking dish on middle rack in oven and broil for 5 minutes. Watch closely. Serve hot.

Makes 2 servings.

PAN-FRIED PEACHES

Use as accompaniment with meat.

Allow one peach per serving. Wash, peel, halve and pit peaches. Melt 2 tablespoons margarine in frypan. Fry over moderately low heat until tender, turning to brown evenly, about 12 to 15 minutes. Sprinkle with 1 tablespoon sugar and ¼ teaspoon cinnamon before serving.

DILLY PEACHES

Marinate fresh peeled peach halves for a half hour in French dressing to which you have added 1 teaspoon dried dill. Drain and pop under the broiler until bubbly. Serve with broiled chicken, baked ham or fish steaks.

S.C. Department of Agriculture

BROILED PEACHES

Good with cured ham or pork!

Peel fresh peaches, halve and remove pit. Place in shallow baking dish. To each half add 1 teaspoon brown sugar, sprinkle with cinnamon and top with ½ teaspoon of margarine. Broil until mixture bubbles and peaches are lightly browned. Serve warm.

PEACH FRITTERS

*Peach fritters are delicious served with any meat dish. They may also
be dusted with confectioners sugar and served as a dessert.*

1	lg	egg
¼	c	whole milk
1-2	c	all-purpose biscuit mix
1	T	lemon juice
2	T	sugar
¼	tsp	ginger
¼	tsp	salt
2	md	peaches, peeled, pitted and diced
		Oil for frying

In a bowl, beat egg, add milk; stir in **1 cup** biscuit mix. Add sugar,
lemon juice, ginger and salt. Stir diced peaches into biscuit mixture.
Add additional biscuit mix as needed until mixture is consistency of thick
pancake mix. In heavy skillet, heat 2 to 3 inches oil to 375° (or use deep
fat fryer). Drop batter into hot oil by teaspoonsful; fry until golden
brown on all sides. Drain on paper towel.

Yield: about 24 fritters.

National Peach Council

PEACH-TUNA CASSEROLE   350° — 30-45 Minutes

2	c	sliced peaches
¼	c	sugar
		Color keeper
2	c	half-and-half
1	c	milk
1	T	inst. minced onion
½		to 1 tsp seafood seasoning
1	tsp	salt
¼	tsp	pepper
2	T	margarine or butter
¾	c	cornmeal
3	lg	eggs
1	can	(13 oz) chunk style tuna, drained*

Gently mix sliced peaches, sugar and color keeper; set aside. Combine half-and-half, milk, minced onion, seafood seasoning, salt and pepper. Heat slowly, stirring constantly, until mixture is hot (do not boil). Stir in margarine and corn meal, remove from heat. Beat eggs in small bowl. Add cornmeal mixture to eggs, a little at a time, stirring constantly, until bowl feels warm to the touch. Slowly stir egg mixture into remaining cornmeal mixture, stirring constantly. Return to heat and stir in tuna. Drain peaches and gently stir into tuna mixture. Heat slowly, stirring constantly, until mixture is hot (do not boil). Pour mixture into greased 2½-3-quart shallow baking dish (or individual casseroles). Bake at 350° until knife inserted in center comes out clean, 30 to 45 minutes. Makes 4 to 6 servings.

*Variation: Substitute one 12-ounce can of fresh or pasteurized Blue crabmeat for tuna; reduce onion to ½ tablespoon and seafood seasoning to ½ teaspoon.

National Peach Council

PORK IN PEACH BOATS   350° — 45 Minutes

1	lb	bulk sausage meat
1½	T	minced onion
2	c	soft bread crumbs
¼	tsp	salt
1/8	tsp	pepper
¼	tsp	commercial flavor enhancer
1		beaten egg
4		peaches, halved
		Whole cloves, if desired

Combine and mix well the sausage, onion, bread crumbs, salt, pepper, flavor enhancer and egg. Form into balls, approximately 1½ inches in diameter. Wash, peel, cut in half and pit the fresh peaches. Arrange in a shallow glass baking dish. Stick with whole cloves, if desired. Place a sausage ball in pit cavity of each peach. Place remaining sausage balls in baking dish. Bake at 350° for 45 minutes. When meat is done, gently remove peaches and sausage balls to a hot platter or drain off excess juices and serve in baking dish. Just before serving pour hot spiced peach syrup* over the peaches and sausage balls.

Makes 4 servings.

*Spiced Peach Syrup: Mix 1 cup sugar, 3 whole cloves, ½ cup vinegar and ½ stick cinnamon and boil for 5 minutes. (Remove cloves and cinnamon before serving.)

Georgia Peach Commission

HAM KABOB WITH PEACH SAUCE

1	c	pureed peaches
½	c	light or dark corn syrup
2	T	lemon juice
2	T	soy sauce
½	tsp	salt
½	tsp	ground ginger OR ¼ tsp tabasco sauce
1/8	tsp	pepper
1	lb	ham steak, cut into 24 pieces
6		peaches, cut into 24 pieces
1		sliced green pepper
1	T	cornstarch
¼	c	cold water

In a medium bowl stir together peach puree, corn syrup, lemon juice, soy sauce, salt, ginger and pepper. Add ham, peaches and green pepper, toss to coat well. Marinate overnight. Arrange peaches, ham and green pepper on eight 8-inch skewers. Baste with some of the remaining sauce. Place on a shallow pan and broil three inches from source of heat for 6-8 minutes turning and basting every 2 minutes. Place remaining peach sauce in a 1-quart saucepan. Stir together cornstarch and water until smooth. Stir into peach mixture, stirring constantly; bring to a boil over medium heat and boil for 1 minute. Serve with Kabobs. (Kabobs may be grilled over hot coals for an outdoor cookout.)
Makes 8 servings.

Georgia Peach Commission

PEACH-HAM KABOBS

¾	c	fresh peach puree
2	T	honey
1	tsp	soy sauce
		Dash of ground cloves
2	lbs	ham (cut into 2-3 inch cubes)
3		green peppers sliced
4		to 5 fresh peaches, peeled or unpeeled* and quartered

Mix peach puree, honey, soy sauce and ground cloves for a marinade sauce. Pour over ham cubes and marinate approximately 15 minutes. Alternate ham cubes, green pepper slices, and fresh peaches on skewers. Broil in broiler or cook over hot coals on a hibachi or an outdoor grill. Brush with marinade sauce as meat cooks.

For a variation: marinade sauce can be poured over wieners in a baking dish and baked at 350° for 15 minutes.

*If used unpeeled, wash thoroughly.

National Peach Council

PEACHYQUE PORK

10		to 12 unpeeled fresh peaches
¼	c	lemon juice
¼	c	soy sauce
⅓	c	honey
1	lg	clove garlic, minced
1/8	tsp	ginger
1/8	tsp	pepper
6	lb	pork roast
1	T	grated lemon rind

Cut **4** or **5** fresh peaches in half; remove pits. Crush or buzz in blender to make 2 cups pulp. Blend **1 cup** pulp with 1 tablespoon of the lemon juice. Cover and refrigerate until needed for sauce. Combine rest of peach pulp, rest of lemon juice, soy sauce, honey, garlic, ginger and pepper into a marinade sauce. Pour over meat. Let stand several hours, turning several times. Drain; save marinade. Secure meat on spit. Cook over low coals about 3 hours; baste often with marinade. Cut rest of peaches in half; remove pits. Lay halves on double thickness of foil. Sprinkle with lemon rind. Brush with marinade. Put on grill under roast about 20 to 30 minutes before roast is done. Serve as garnish with roast. Add reserved 1 cup peach pulp/lemon juice mixture to remaining marinade. Heat and serve with meat.

Makes 12 servings. *S.C. Department of Agriculture*

MAPLE HAM PEACHES

A touch of New England!

1		egg, beaten
½	c	soft bread crumbs
½	c	maple syrup
1/8	tsp	ground cloves
1	tsp	prepared mustard
1	lb	cooked ham, ground
12		peach halves, fresh or canned
		Parsley to garnish, optional
		Additional maple syrup

Combine egg, crumbs, syrup, cloves, mustard and ham. Shape into 12 balls. Drain peach halves and place a ham ball in the center of each. Bake at 350° for 25 minutes in a greased shallow baking dish. Baste once or twice with additional maple syrup to prevent drying out. Five minutes before baking time is up, garnish with chopped parsley if desired.

Yield: 12 peach halves.

SAUCY PEACH-SPICED CHICKEN

Good served over rice!

		Cooking oil to depth of ½-inch in large skillet
½	c	flour mixed with 1 tsp salt and 1/8 tsp pepper
6		each fryer chicken legs & thighs
	OR	
1		ready-to-cook chicken
	OR	
2		breasts & 4 thighs disjointed
1	c	orange juice
1½	c	sliced peaches, fresh, canned or frozen
2	T	brown sugar
2	T	vinegar
1	tsp	mace OR nutmeg
1	tsp	sweet basil
1		clove garlic, minced

Put oil in fry pan. While it is heating dredge chicken in seasoned flour. Brown chicken. While it is browning, combine orange juice and peaches with brown sugar, vinegar, mace or nutmeg, sweet basil and minced garlic. Simmer 10 minutes. Remove chicken when it is browned and pour off oil, retaining the flavory browned bits in skillet. Replace chicken and pour fruit sauce over top. Cover and simmer about 20 minutes.

Makes 4 to 6 servings.

South Carolina Peach Council

BAKED PEACHES AND SAUSAGE

450° — 15 Minutes
+ 15 Minutes

1	lb	mild bulk pork sausage
1	can	(29 oz) peach halves
¼	c	brown sugar, firmly packed
½	tsp	ground cinnamon
¼	tsp	ground cloves

Cook sausage until browned, stirring to crumble. Drain well on paper towels and set aside. Drain peach halves, reserving ¼ cup juice. Place peaches, cut side up, in a well-greased 10x6x2-inch glass baking dish; add reserved juice. Combine brown sugar and spices, stirring well; sprinkle over peach halves. Bake at 450° for 15 minutes; remove from oven and sprinkle cooked sausage evenly over top. Return to oven and bake 15 minutes.

Makes 6 servings.

CURRIED HAM STEAK   350° — 30 Minutes

2		smoked ham slices (½-inch thick)
1	can	(17 oz) peach halves, drained
1	can	(16 oz) pear halves, drained
1	can	(15¼ oz) pineapple slices, drained
¼	c	raisins
¼	c	butter or margarine
¼	c	brown sugar, firmly packed
1	T	curry powder

Place ham steaks in a 13x9x2-inch baking dish. Arrange fruit evenly over the ham. Melt butter in a small saucepan, and stir in brown sugar and curry. Pour sauce over fruit. Bake at 350° for 30 minutes or until thoroughly heated.

Makes 6 servings.

HAM AND PEACH CURRIE

1	can	(16 oz) peach halves
1	T	butter or margarine
4		slices cooked ham
1	tsp	curry powder
2	T	brown sugar
1	T	butter or margarine

Drain peach halves, reserving syrup. Set aside. Melt 1 tablespoon butter in a large skillet. Brown ham in butter; remove and set aside. Add peach syrup and curry powder to pan drippings. Place peach halves, cut side down, in syrup mixture; cook over medium heat 2 minutes. Turn peaches; fill cavities with brown sugar, and dot with remaining butter. Return ham to skillet; cover and cook 3 minutes.

Makes 4 servings.

HARVEST MEATBALLS   350° — 30 Minutes

1		egg, beaten
¼	c	milk
¾	c	soft bread crumbs
¼	c	chopped onion
½	tsp	EACH ground cinnamon and salt
		Dash of pepper
½	lb	ground beef
½	lb	bulk pork sausage
1½	c	chicken broth
¾	c	long grain rice
2	T	parsley, snipped
¼	c	butter or margarine
¼	c	brown sugar, packed
1½	c	peeled and sliced peaches
1	T	cornstarch
¼	c	cold water
¼	c	lemon juice
¼	c	sliced almonds

Combine egg and milk. Stir in crumbs, onion, ¼ teaspoon of the cinnamon, salt and dash of pepper. Add meats; mix well. Shape into 20 meatballs. Place in shallow baking pan. Bake, uncovered, 350° for 30 minutes. Drain. Meanwhile, combine broth, rice, parsley and remaining cinnamon. Bring to boiling. Cover and simmer about 15 minutes. Melt butter; stir in brown sugar. Add peaches; cook about 2 minutes. Combine cornstarch and ¼ cup cold water. Stir into fruit mixture. Cook and stir till bubbly. Stir in lemon juice. Serve meatballs over rice; spoon fruit sauce over. Sprinkle with almonds.

Makes 4 servings.

PEACH GLAZE FOR BARBEQUE

4	T	butter
¼	tsp	EACH of mace, sweet basil and ground nutmeg
1	tsp	salt
1	T	brown sugar
1	c	peach puree
2	T	frozen orange juice concentrate
2	T	lemon juice

Melt butter and add the spices, salt and sugar. Heat only until well blended. Mix puree, orange juice and lemon juice and add to spice mixture. Heat again only enough to blend the mixture to a smooth sauce. Use as any barbeque sauce over chicken, pork chops or ham on grill or in oven.

National Peach Council

QUICK AND EASY PEACH LEATHER

Puree fully ripe peaches in blender until very smooth. Add 2 teaspoons ascorbic acid powder and 2 tablespoons of sugar per quart of puree if desired. Heat just to boiling to dissolve sugar and to prevent darkening. Lightly oil or spray with non-stick coating a jelly roll pan or cookie sheet with low sides. Spread puree thinly on pans (about ¼-inch thick). Bake in a 150° oven for 4-6 hours or until no longer tacky to the touch. Run knife around edges and peel out of the pan. Roll up or cut if desired. May be stored in an airtight container for several weeks at room temperature, several months in the refrigerator or several years in the freezer.

PEACH PUREE

2	c	sliced peaches
½	c	sugar
		Color keeper or lemon juice
		Pinch of salt

Place all ingredients into blender container. Blend until smooth. May be frozen if desired in 1 or 2 cup portions. May be used in recipes, or as a topping for ice cream or pancakes.

Makes 1 pint.

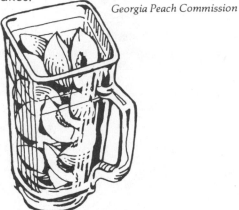

Georgia Peach Commission

FRUIT DRESSINGS

Spicy Nectar Dressing:

In small mixer bowl combine 1 cup dairy sour cream, ½ cup apricot nectar, ½ cup salad oil, 2 tablespoons sugar, ½ teaspoon ground cinnamon, ½ teaspoon paprika, and dash salt. Beat till smooth. Cover and chill. Serve with fresh peaches.

Yield: 2 cups.

Strawberry-Cheese Dressing:

In small mixer bowl combine one 3-ounce package cream cheese, softened; ½ of a 10-ounce package frozen strawberries, thawed; 1 tablespoon sugar; 1 tablespoon lemon juice; and dash salt. Beat till smooth. Add ½ cup salad oil in a slow stream, beating till thick. Cover and chill. Serve with fresh peaches.

Yield: 1½ cups.

Heavenly Fruit Dip:

Combine ½ cup sugar, 2 tablespoons all-purpose flour, 1 cup pineapple juice, 1 egg, beaten, and 1 tablespoon butter in a heavy saucepan; cook over medium heat, stirring constantly, until smooth and thickened. Let cool completely; fold in 1 cup whipped cream. Serve with fresh peaches.

Yield: about 2 cups.

CREAMY FRESH PEACH SOUP

*Serve, with crackers, and you have
an appetizer fit for a queen!*

2	T	butter
1½	T	flour
¼	tsp	salt
1	c	half and half
1¼	c	peach puree
1	T	sugar

Melt butter in medium size sauce pan. Mix in flour and salt and heat until bubbly. Add the half and half and the peach puree that has been sweetened with the tablespoon of sugar. Cook over low to moderate heat, stirring constantly, until thick. Serve warm or cold. A garnish might be a dollop of whipped cream or sour cream. (Soup can be made a day ahead of time and stored in the refrigerator.)

Makes about 4 servings.

National Peach Council

SEASONAL FRUIT SOUP

*Serve this soup in pretty chilled crystal or glass bowls
for your next special occasion.*

¼	c	sugar
2	T	cornstarch
1¾	c	apple juice
1	can	(12 oz) apricot nectar
4		inches stick cinnamon
4		whole cloves
3	c	peeled and sliced peaches
½	c	unsweetened white grape juice

In large saucepan combine sugar and cornstarch. Stir in apple juice, apricot nectar, stick cinnamon and cloves. Cook and stir till thickened and bubbly, reduce heat. Cover and simmer for 15 minutes, stirring occasionally. Remove from heat. Stir in peaches and grape juice. Cover and chill overnight. Remove cinnamon and cloves; stir well before serving. Serve in chilled bowls.
Makes 6 servings.

We are only certain of today...yesterday is gone and tomorrow is always coming.

Martin Vanbee

FRESH PEACH-SQUASH CASSEROLE   350° — 45-60 Minutes

2½	c	sliced soft-skinned squash (yellow crookneck or zuccini)
1	c	fresh sliced peaches
2	T	brown sugar
		Salt to taste
2½	T	butter

Place layer of squash then layer of peaches in a 2-quart casserole. Continue alternating layers of fruit and vegetable until all have been used. Sprinkle brown sugar and salt over the combination and dot with butter. Cover and bake at 350° for 45 minutes to 1 hour.
Makes 4 servings.

National Peach Council

PEACHY GREEN BEANS

2	lbs	fresh green beans, cut into 1-inch pieces*
1½	tsp	salt
½	c	slivered almonds
¼	c	melted butter
3	md	peaches, sliced
		Lemon juice

Bring four cups of water to a boil. Add green beans and salt. Cook for 8 minutes or until beans are tender; drain. Saute almonds in butter. Add peach slices; saute slightly. Sprinkle lightly with lemon juice. Gently toss with green beans.

Makes 6 to 8 servings.

*Three cans (16 ounces each) cut green beans can be used in place of fresh green beans. Omit salt. Heat beans until boiling; drain. Proceed with recipe.

National Peach Council

SUNSHINE LIMAS

1	pt	fresh shelled lima beans*
2	T	onion, chopped
¼	c	butter, melted
3	T	flour
1	tsp	curry powder
1	c	whole milk
5		to 6 medium peaches, sliced
3	T	butter, melted
		Curry powder

Cook beans until tender; drain. Place in 9x11-inch baking dish. Saute onion in butter until translucent. Add flour and 1 teaspoon curry powder, stirring until smooth. Gradually add milk; stirring until thickened. Pour sauce over beans and gently toss. Arrange peach slices on top of bean mixture. Brush with 3 tablespoons butter. Sprinkle with curry powder. Serve immediately.

Makes 8 to 10 servings.

*Two 10-ounce packages of frozen lima beans can be used in place of fresh beans.

National Peach Council

FRESH PEACH SURPRISES

1		egg
½*	c	whole milk*
¾	c	flour (approx)
½	tsp	salt
1	tsp	baking powder
		Fresh peaches
		Cinnamon
		Powdered sugar
		Vegetable oil

Beat egg and milk well, add flour, salt and baking powder. Peel peaches and halve them; dip into batter and fry slowly in vegetable oil. Dust with powdered sugar and a little cinnamon. *(May need a little more milk.)

South Carolina Department of Agriculture

SANDWICH PEACHES

6		fresh peaches, unpeeled
2	pkg	(3 oz each) cream cheese, softened
¾	c	finely chopped boiled ham
3	T	finely chopped pecans
6		wooden skewers

Halve and pit peaches. Cut each half again, lengthwise, to make 4 round slices per peach. Dry cut sides with paper towels. In bowl, blend cream cheese, ham and nuts. Sandwich peach slices back together with ham mixture, using about 3 tablespoons per peach. Press gently. Wrap in plastic wrap. Chill 4 hours or overnight. To serve, cut each peach crosswise into 3 slices. Insert wooden skewer through slices, if necessary, to hold layers together.

Makes 6 servings.

California Tree Fruit Agreement

PEACHY GRAHAM SNACKS

2	T	margarine, softened
1	c	powdered sugar
1	T	mashed fresh peaches
		Graham Crackers

Cream margarine and sugar until smooth. Add mashed fresh peaches and mix. (If filling is not stiff enough to spread, add more powdered sugar.) Spread filling over graham cracker and top with second graham cracker. These may be wrapped in foil and chilled to firm.

National Peach Council

PEACH POPSICLES

6	lg	ripe peaches
¾	c	sugar
½	c	water
2	T	lemon juice
1	pkg	unflavored gelatin
1	c	lukewarm water
		Pinch of salt

Puree peaches with sugar, ½ cup water and lemon juice in blender. Dissolve gelatin in 1 cup lukewarm water and add to blender container. Add pinch of salt. Blend until smooth. Pour into 14 small paper cups. Freeze until firm. Roll in hands then push up from the bottom to eat.

Georgia Peach Commission

Makes 14 servings.

GRILLED PEACHES AND BERRIES

Large ripe peaches (allow 1 half per serving)
Fresh or frozen blueberries
Brown sugar
Lemon juice

Wash, peel, pit and halve peaches. Place each half on a double thickness of heavy duty aluminum foil. Fill the peach half generously with fresh or frozen blueberries. Sprinkle with 2 teaspoons brown sugar and 1 teaspoon lemon juice on each. Wrap securely. Cook on grill 18-20 minutes turning once. Serve right out of the foil. These can also be baked in the oven; bake in foil or glass dish at 350° for about 15 minutes or until peaches are done.

Georgia Peach Commission

BAKED FRUIT MEDLEY   325°—30 Minutes

1		orange
1		lemon
1	can	(16 oz) sliced peaches, drained
1	can	(16 oz) pear halves, drained
1	can	(16 oz) apricots, drained
1	can	(15½ oz) sliced pineapple, drained
1	jar	(6 oz) maraschino cherries, drained
1	c	brown sugar, firmly packed
1	T	all-purpose flour

Grate rind of orange and lemon; peel and slice. Layer orange and lemon slices and remaining fruit in a 13x9x2-inch baking dish. Combine orange and lemon rind, brown sugar, flour and bitters; mix well and sprinkle over fruit. Bake at 325° for 30 minutes or until bubbly. Serve hot or chilled.
Makes 12 to 14 servings.

Perfection consists not in doing extraordinary things, but in doing ordinary things extraordinarily well.

Antoine Arnauld

BAKED FRUIT COMPOTE   425°—15-20 Minutes

1	can	(16 oz) peach halves, drained
1	can	(16 oz) apricot halves, drained
1	can	(16 oz) whole purple plums, drained
3		or 4 thin orange slices, halved
½	c	orange juice
¼	c	brown sugar, firmly packed
½	t	grated lemon rind
2	T	butter or margarine, melted
½	c	flaked coconut

Alternate rows of peaches, apricots and plums in a 12x7½x1½-inch baking dish. Place half an orange slice between each peach. Combine orange juice, brown sugar and lemon rind; mix well and pour over fruit. Spoon butter over plums; sprinkle coconut over all fruit. Bake at 425° for 15 to 20 minutes or until coconut is toasted.
Makes 8 to 10 servings.

Two variations of that tasty menu addition, curried fruit.

CURRIED FRUIT   350°—1 Hour

1	can	(16 oz) peach halves
1	can	(16 oz) pear halves
1	can	(20 oz) pineapple chunks
1		sm bottle maraschino cherries
2/3		stick butter, melted
¾	c	light brown sugar, packed
2-4	tsp	curry powder

Drain the peaches, pears, pineapple and cherries and place in a 1½-quart casserole. Mix the butter, sugar and curry powder and spoon over fruits in casserole. Bake, covered, at 350° for 1 hour.

Makes 6 to 8 servings.

HOT CURRIED FRUIT   325°—30 Minutes

1	can	(16 oz) peach halves
1	can	(16 oz) sliced pears
1	can	(15 oz) pineapple chunks
1	can	(16 oz) apricot halves
1	jar	(6 oz) maraschino cherries
1	can	(16 oz) pitted dark sweet cherries
1	c	brown sugar, firmly packed
1	T	curry powder
¼	c	butter or margarine
¼	t	ground cinnamon
1/8	t	EACH ground nutmeg and salt
1	T	lemon juice

Drain fruit and pat dry with paper towels; place in a 13x9x2-inch baking dish. Sprinkle with brown sugar and curry powder, and mix gently; dot with butter. Sprinkle with remaining ingredients. Refrigerate several hours or overnight. Remove from refrigerator 15 minutes before baking. Bake at 325° for 30 minutes.

Makes 8 to 10 servings.

FRUIT MACEDOINE 250°—1 Hour

1	can	(29 oz) peach halves
1	can	(20 oz) sliced pineapple
1	can	(29 oz) pear halves
1	can	(16 oz) apricot halves
1	can	(16 oz) applesauce
		Butter
		Ginger to taste

Drain the peaches, pineapple, pears and apricots and place in a large baking dish. Cover with applesauce and dot with butter. Sprinkle with ginger. Bake at 250° for 1 hour.

SPICED FRUIT DELIGHT

*Especially pretty served in a large "brandy sniffer"
or individual glass bowls.*

4	c	unsweetened apple juice
2		to 3 (3-inch) cinnamon sticks
2	t	lemon juice
2		peaches, peeled and cut into thin wedges
2		apples, cored and cut into thin wedges
2		pears, cored and cut into thin wedges
¼	lb	cherries, pitted
2	c	fresh strawberries, hulled

Combine apple juice and cinnamon in a saucepan; bring to a boil. Boil 10 minutes; cool. Add lemon juice and all fruit except strawberries. Chill. Stir in strawberries just before serving.

Makes 8 servings.

GINGERED BAKED FRUIT   325°—30 Minutes

1	can	(20 oz) pineapple chunks, drained
1	can	(16 oz) pear halves, drained
1	can	(16 oz) peach halves, drained
1	jar	(6 oz) maraschino cherries, drained
¼	c	butter or margarine
¾	c	brown sugar, firmly packed
1	T	ground ginger

Combine fruit in a 1½-quart casserole. Melt butter; add sugar and ginger, stirring until smooth. Pour ginger mixture over fruit. Bake at 325° for 30 minutes.

Makes 8 servings.

HOT FRUIT COMPOTE   300°—1 Hour

The applesauce makes the difference!

1	can	(16 oz) sliced peaches, drained
1	can	(16 oz) pear halves, drained and coarsely chopped
1	can	(16 oz) whole purple plums, drained and pitted
1	can	(20 oz) pineapple chunks, drained
1	jar	(6 oz) maraschino cherries, drained
2		bananas, sliced
¾	c	plus 3 tablespoons brown sugar, firmly packed
⅓	c	butter or margarine
1	can	(16 oz) applesauce
½	c	chopped pecans

Combine peaches, pears, plums, pineapple, cherries and bananas in a 13x9x2-inch baking dish; set dish aside. Combine ¾ **cup** brown sugar, butter and applesauce in saucepan; heat thoroughly, stirring occasionally. Spoon applesauce mixture over fruit; sprinkle with 3 tablespoons brown sugar and pecans. Bake at 300° for 1 hour. Serve hot. Compote may be prepared ahead; cover baking dish with plastic wrap and freeze. To serve, let thaw overnight in refrigerator and bake according to directions.

Makes 10 to 12 servings.

GLAZED CORNED BEEF AND PEACHES
(main dish)

325°F
2 hrs + 30 Minutes
+ 10-15 Minutes

A nice change from the ordinary!

1		3-lb corned beef brisket
2	c	water
6		fresh peaches, peeled & halved
	OR	
1	can	(29 oz) peach halves, drained
½	c	peach preserves
¼	tsp	ground ginger

Rinse brisket in cold water to remove pickling juices. Place, fat side up, on rack in shallow roasting pan. Add water; cover with foil. Roast in 325° oven for 2 hours. Uncover, drain cooking liquid, reserving ½ cup liquid in pan. Arrange peach halves, cut side down, around corned beef in roasting pan. Return to oven; continue roasting, uncovered, for 30 minutes more. For glaze, combine peach preserves and ginger. Turn peach halves cut side up. Spoon glaze over peaches and corned beef. Return to oven and roast for 10 to 15 minutes more till glaze is heated through.

Makes 6 to 8 servings.

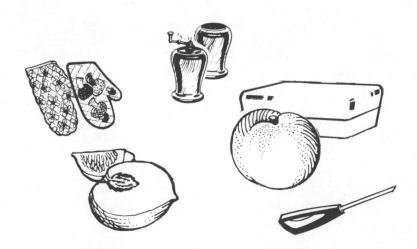

Recipes

For Microwave, Nectarines and Calorie Conscious

Keeping fit is a national pasttime and sociable activity today. These low-calorie keep-fit recipes are a delicious way to help maintain a slim life.

Microwave cooking is versatile and fast for the modern on-the-go cook. Microwave cooking not only saves time but also saves energy leaving the cook unhurried and unworried with more time for family and friends.

A book of peach recipes would not be complete without including recipes for nectarines. Here is a selection of recipes which even the nectarine connoisseur will appreciate.

PRETTY PEACH PARFAITS

1	env	(1 T) unflavored gelatin
¼	c	cold water
1¼	c	buttermilk
1	T	lemon juice
		Sugar substitute equivalent to ½ c sugar
¾	tsp	almond extract
		Yellow food coloring
3		peaches, sliced

Soften the gelatin in cold water in a saucepan. Place over low heat and stir until gelatin is dissolved. Remove from heat and add the buttermilk, lemon juice, sweetener, almond extract and several drops of food coloring. Chill until mixture is consistency of unbeaten egg whites. Layer the gelatin mixture and peaches in 3 tall glasses, using about 2/3 cup gelatin mixture in each glass, and chill until firm.

Makes 3 servings.

TASTY PEACH BUTTER

1	can	(16 oz) peaches, juice pack
1	env	(1 T) unflavored gelatin
½	c	unsweetened apple juice

Drain peaches and reserve juice; place 2 tablespoons of the juice in blender container. Sprinkle gelatin over the juice. Bring apple juice to a boil; when gelatin has softened, pour the apple juice into the blender container. Process on high speed until gelatin has dissolved. Add the peaches and remaining peach juice; process until smooth and fluffy. Chill until set.

Yield: 2½ cups at less than 7 calories per tablespoon.

SURPRISE PEACH JAM

4	c	peeled peaches
3-4	tsp	liquid artificial sweetener
1	pkg	(1¾ oz) powdered fruit pectin
1	T	unsweetened lemon juice
½	tsp	ascorbic acid

Crush peaches in saucepan. Stir in sweetener, fruit pectin, lemon juice and ascorbic acid. Bring to a boil, boil 1 minute. Remove from heat. Continue to stir 2 minutes. Pour into freezer containers. Cover; freeze.

Yield: about 1 pint with 10 calories per tablespoon.

SPECIAL PEACH ICE CREAM

1	qt	thin-sliced peaches
2	c	sugar
7	c	whole milk
2/3	c	corn syrup
1½	c	non-fat dry milk solids
1	pkg	(sm) instant vanilla pudding

Wash thoroughly and slice soft ripe peaches; blend with about 1 cup sugar. Let stand ½ hour. Mix together milk, 1 cup sugar, corn syrup, dry milk and pudding; pour into ice cream freezer and freeze until partially frozen. Open and add peach mixture; continue freezing according to manufacturer's directions until firm.

COOLING PEACH ICE CREAM

2	c	peeled and crushed peaches
1	c	sugar
1½	T	lemon juice
1	tsp	ascorbic acid powder
½	tsp	vanilla
¼	tsp	almond extract
1	c	instant non-fat dry milk solids
1	c	ice water

Crush peaches. Add sugar, lemon juice, ascorbic acid powder, vanilla and almond extract. Stir to dissolve sugar. Whip instant milk and water in 2-quart bowl with rotary beater or electric mixer until soft peaks form. Fold whipped milk into peach mixture. Pour into two 1-quart ice trays. Freeze. When frozen, turn mixture into a 2-quart bowl and beat until smooth and creamy, but not melted. Return to ice trays and refreeze.
Makes 8 servings.

S.C. Department of Agriculture

CHEESECAKE COUSIN

Stir non-caloric sweetener and a dash of vanilla into small curd cottage cheese. Spoon into the center of fresh peach halves. Sprinkle with graham cracker crumbs mixed with a little melted butter and a dash of cinnamon; cheese cake goodness without the calories!

South Carolina Department of Agriculture

THICK PEACH SHAKE

½	c	sliced peaches
½	c	skimmed milk
1		individual pkg artificial sweetener
2		drops almond flavoring, if desired
4		to 8 ice cubes, cracked

Process peaches, milk, sweetener and flavoring in a blender. Add ice cubes one at a time and blend at a high speed. The drink will be quite thick. Twelve ounces has only 75 calories.

Georgia Peach Commission

FRESH PEACH MELBA FLOAT

3		fresh peaches, peeled and sliced
1		banana, sliced
1	pt	raspberry sherbet
		Diet ginger ale

Arrange peach and banana slices in 6 stemmed glasses. Top with a scoop of sherbet. Set glasses in freezer 15 minutes to frost. To serve, fill glasses with ginger ale; accompany with straw and spoon.
Yield: 6 drinks. (127 calories per drink)

California Tree Fruit Agreement

BAKED PEACH MELBA

1	c	unsweetened orange juice
1	tsp	sugar substitute
¼	tsp	allspice
3	lg	fresh peaches, peeled and halved
2	T	dietetic raspberry preserves

Combine orange juice, sweetener and allspice in an 8x8x2-inch baking dish. Microwave on **High** for 3 to 4 minutes or until juice is boiling. Arrange peaches in baking dish with sauce. Spoon sauce over peaches. Microwave on **High** for 4 to 6 minutes or until peaches are tender. Turn peaches, cut side up, top with warm liquid and 1 teaspoon of preserves.
Makes 4 to 6 servings.

QUICK PEACH COBBLER

2	cans	(29 oz ea) peach slices, drain and reserve ¼ c syrup
3	T	flour
½	T	lemon juice
½	tsp	vanilla extract
½	tsp	ground cinnamon
1	c	buttermilk biscuit mix
¼	c	brown sugar
¼	c	butter or margarine, softened
2	T	hot water

In square baking dish, combine peaches, flour, lemon juice, vanilla extract, and cinnamon. In another bowl combine biscuit mix, brown sugar, butter and hot water, stirring until dough pulls away from sides of bowl and forms a ball. Gently spread topping onto filling (topping will spread slightly when heated). Sprinkle, if desired, with additional cinnamon. Cook at **Medium-High** for 9 to 11 minutes or until topping is set. Let stand to cool.

DELUXE PEACHY COFFEE CAKE

1		egg
1	c	flour
1	c	brown sugar, packed
⅓	c	half 'n half
¼	c	oil
1	tsp	vanilla extract
½	tsp	salt
½	tsp	baking powder
½	tsp	cinnamon
¼	tsp	nutmeg
1	can	(16 oz) sliced peaches, drained & chopped
¼	c	flaked coconut
¼	c	chopped walnuts
2	T	old-fashioned or quick oats
2	T	butter or margarine, softened

In large bowl, with electric mixer, blend eggs, flour, 2/3 cup sugar, half 'n half, oil, vanilla, salt, baking powder, cinnamon and nutmeg. Beat at low speed ½ minute; at medium speed 1 minute. Fold in peaches. Pour batter into a greased 9-inch round cake dish with a greased small glass inverted in center. In small bowl, combine coconut, nuts, ⅓ cup brown sugar and oats. Cut in butter until it resembles coarse crumbs. Sprinkle over batter. Cook at **Medium** for 14 minutes. Let stand, covered, 5 minutes.

BAKED PEACH MELBA

1	c	unsweetened orange juice
1	tsp	sugar substitute
¼	tsp	allspice
3	lg	fresh peaches, peeled and halved
2	T	dietetic raspberry preserves

Combine orange juice, sweetner and allspice in an 8x8x2-inch baking dish. Microwave on **High** for 3 to 4 minutes or until juice is boiling. Arrange peaches in baking dish with sauce. Spoon sauce over peaches. Microwave on **High** for 4 to 6 minutes or until peaches are tender. Turn peaches, cut side up, top with warm liquid and 1 teaspoon of preserves.
   Makes 4 to 6 servings.

Happiness is best attained by learning to live each day by itself. The worries are mostly about yesterday and tomorrow.

Michael Nolan

PEACHY PORK ROAST

		Water
1	can	(8 oz) sliced peaches, drained & chopped (reserve syrup)
1	pkg	(6 oz) stuffing mix for pork
1		egg
⅓	c	chopped walnuts
¼	c	butter or margarine
3	lb	pork roast
¼	c	peach preserves

In 2-cup glass measure, add enough water to reserved syrup to equal 1½ cups. Heat on **High** power for 2 to 3 minutes or until hot. In medium glass bowl, combine liquid with peaches, stuffing mix (and include seasoning packet), egg, walnuts and butter. Stir until liquid is absorbed and butter melted. Cut pockets in pork roast and stuff each pocket with 2 tablespoons stuffing; secure with string or wooden toothpicks. In small bowl place leftover stuffing and reserve. In a 2-quart oblong baking dish arrange roast on microwave-safe cooking rack. Cook at **Medium** for 11 to 13 minutes **per pound.** Halfway through heating, brush on preserves. When done, let stand, covered, 15 minutes. Meanwhile, heat remaining stuffing at **Medium-Low** for 6 to 7 minutes, stir twice.

FAST PEACH PIE

2	lbs	fresh peaches, peeled and sliced
½	c	brown sugar
1½	T	cornstarch
2	tsp	lemon juice
½	tsp	ground cinnamon, optional
1		9-inch pastry shell, baked
		Crumb Topping*

Toss peaches with sugar, cornstarch, lemon juice and cinnamon; arrange in prepared shell. Heat, covered with wax paper, 4 to 6 minutes or until peaches are almost tender. Sprinkle with Crumb Topping; heat 4 to 5 minutes at **High** or until topping is set. Let stand until cool.

*Crumb Topping: Combine ½ cup flour, ⅓ cup brown sugar, ¼ cup butter or margarine, softened, ¼ teaspoon ground cinnamon, and ⅓ cup finely chopped nuts, optional.

COMPOTE OF CURRIED FRUIT

1	can	(17 oz) apricot halves, drain and reserve syrup
1	can	(16 oz) peach slices, drain and reserve syrup
¼	tsp	curry powder
¼	tsp	ground cinnamon
1	T	cornstarch
¼	c	water
½	c	raisins

In 2-cup glass measure, combine 1 cup reserved syrups, curry and cinnamon; heat 2 to 3 minutes. Stir in cornstarch blended with water and heat 1½ to 2 minutes or until slightly thickened, stirring occasionally. In baking dish, combine apricots, peaches and raisins; heat 3½ to 4½ minutes or until heated through, stirring once. Pour in sauce and heat 1 to 1½ minutes. Serve warm or chilled.

EASY-TO-PREPARE PEACHES

Melt about 2 - 3 tablespoons margarine in a glass dish. Add brown sugar OR pancake syrup OR honey OR some other sweetener. Sprinkle in a little cinnamon and nutmeg. Add peach halves (fresh or canned) and drizzle mixture over halves. Microwave until slightly warm (2 - 3 minutes). May add a dollop of sour cream or jam to each half. Serve around meat or serve warm with whipped cream as a dessert.

S.C. Department of Agriculture

EASY SPICED PEACHES

2		cans (29 oz ea) peach halves
2	T	cider vinegar
1	tsp	whole allspice
1	tsp	whole cloves
4		cinnamon sticks

Drain peaches well, reserving 1½ cups syrup. In 2-quart bowl, combine reserved syrup, vinegar, allspice, cloves and cinnamon sticks. Microwave 4 to 6 minutes on **high,** or until mixture boils. Reduce setting, microwave 4 minutes on **"6".** Remove and discard cloves. Arrange peach halves in 12x8-inch baking dish. Pour hot syrup over peaches. Microwave 5 minutes on **"6",** basting peaches several times. Serve hot or cold. Peaches will keep in jars several days, refrigerated.

Yield: 2 to 3 pints.

HONEY BAKED PEACHES

4		fresh ripe peaches, peeled and halved
	OR	
8		canned peach halves
¼	c	water
⅓	c	honey
2	T	lemon juice
		Dash of cinnamon
		Coconut, optional

Arrange peach halves in an 8x8x2-inch baking dish. Combine water, honey, lemon juice and cinnamon. Pour over peaches. Cover with a tight fitting lid or plastic wrap. Microwave fresh peaches on **High** for 5 to 8 minutes or until peaches are tender (stir halfway through cooking) OR microwave canned peaches 3 to 4 minutes or until heated through. Sprinkle with coconut. Serve warm or cold.

Makes 8 servings.

HURRY-UP PEACH JAM

4	c	fresh peeled and sliced peaches
7¼	c	sugar
¼	c	lemon juice
1		pouch (3 oz) liquid pectin

In large glass bowl, combine peaches, sugar and lemon juice. Heat 15 to 17 minutes on **high** or until mixture comes to a full boil, stirring occasionally during the first 5 minutes. Heat an additional 1 minute. Stir in pectin and skim off any foam; stir and skim foam for about 7 minutes. Ladle into glasses; seal with paraffin.

YUMMY PEACHY MUFFINS

1	can	(8 oz) sliced peaches, drained (reserve ¼ cup syrup)
⅓	c	brown sugar
3	T	butter or margarine
1		egg
1	c	flour
½	c	chopped pecans
1	tsp	baking powder
½	tsp	salt

Finely chop ¼ cup peaches; set aside. Cream together remaining peaches, sugar and butter; stir in egg and reserved syrup. Add flour, pecans, baking powder and salt, stirring only until flour is moistened; stir in the ¼ cup chopped peaches. Fill 6 custard cups (6 oz each), lined with cupcake paper liners, 2/3 full; arrange in circular pattern on glass oven tray (or use a microwave-safe cupcake pan). Heat 4½ to 5½ minutes at **Medium-Low;** repeat procedure with remaining batter, filling 3 cups. Heat 2½ to 3 minutes. Let stand 5 minutes; store, covered, until ready to serve.

MILD PEACH CHUTNEY

1	lg	unpeeled apple, cored and chopped
1	c	chopped celery
¼	c	chopped green pepper
1	T	finely chopped onion
2	cans	(16 oz ea) sliced peaches
½	c	seedless raisins
¾	c	cider vinegar
½	c	sugar
½	tsp	salt
¼	tsp	ginger
		Dash cayenne pepper

Combine all ingredients in 3-quart casserole, stir well and cover. Microwave 5 minutes on **high,** or **until mixture boils.** Reduce setting. Microwave 45 minutes on "5", or until syrup is thickened and chutney is desired consistency, stirring 2 or 3 times. Ladle into hot sterilized jars. Cover tightly. Cool. Store in refrigerator and serve with meats.

Yield: 2 pints.

SPICY PEACH UP-SIDE DOWN CAKE

3	T	butter or margarine
¼	c	brown sugar
1/8	c	chopped nuts
		sugar, cinnamon & nutmeg
2	c	sliced fresh peaches
1	pkg	(18.5 oz) spice cake mix plus
		ingredients called for on package

Melt margarine in 8-inch round glass cake pan. Spread brown sugar over margarine. Sprinkle with nuts. Sprinkle sugar, cinnamon and nutmeg over sliced peaches, stir to coat slices. Spread peaches over nuts. Pour in **2 cups** of cake batter. Cook on medium 4 minutes, rotate dish ½ turn. Cook on high about 2 - 3 minutes. Let stand a few minutes, invert cake on plate. (One 18.5 oz cake mix will make 2 up-side down cakes with extra batter for cupcakes.)
Makes 6 servings.

S.C. Department of Agriculture

CRUNCHY PEACH CRISP

6	c	fresh sliced peaches
		sugar, cinnamon, nutmeg
½	c	unsifted all-purpose flour
½	c	quick cooking rolled oats
¾	c	brown sugar, packed
1	tsp	cinnamon
¼	c	butter or margarine

Sprinkle peaches with sugar, cinnamon and nutmeg. Place in 2-quart glass baking dish. Combine flour, oats, brown sugar and 1 teaspoon cinnamon in medium mixing bowl. Cut in butter until crumbly. Sprinkle over peaches. Microwave on **high** 4 minutes. Rotate dish ½ turn. Cook 3 - 4 minutes longer. Serve warm or cold with ice cream or whipped cream.
Makes 6 to 8 servings.

S.C. Department of Agriculture

RAISIN-PEACH CONSERVE

3	c	(16 oz ea) canned peaches, chopped
1		orange, peeled and chopped
½	c	raisins
2	T	lemon juice
1	pkg	(1¾ oz) powdered pectin
5	c	sugar
1	c	walnuts, chopped

Combine peaches, orange, raisins, lemon juice and pectin in a 3-quart casserole. Cover loosely with lid or plastic wrap. Microwave on **High** for 5 to 6 minutes or until mixture comes to a full boil. Stir occasionally during cooking. Stir in sugar until dissolved. Cover. Microwave on **High** for 8 to 10 minutes or until mixture again comes to a full boil. Stir occasionally during cooking. Uncover. Microwave on **High** for an additional 2 to 3 minutes or until mixture sheets from a spoon. Skim off foam. Stir in walnuts. Allow to stand 5 minutes. Pour into hot sterilized jars. Seal.

Yield: 6 half-pints.

Since canned peaches are used, this can be made for Winter Holiday meals and gift giving.

The nectarine is probably an ancestor of the peach and like other stone fruits is a member of the rose family. Nectarines look and taste like a peach without "fuzz." They are red, white or yellow-fleshed and can be freestone or clingstone.

Profile of a nectarine:

Shape — round to oblong, well-formed and plump shoulders near stem end, hemispheres equal and well-shaped.

Skin — thin, smooth, waxy, tender and fuzzless.

Color — creamy to yellow background, blushed with crimson, sometimes freckled.

Flesh — white or yellow, firm juicy, may be bright red at pit, freestone or clingstone.

Flavor — sweet with slight tartness in skin, aromatic and reminescent of rose fragrance.

Peeling isn't necessary but if desired, submerge into boiling water for about 30 seconds; then dip immediately in cold water and the skin will slip right off. As with peaches, to prevent discoloration when peeled or cut, dip or sprinkle with ascorbic acid, commercial color keeper or citrus juice.

One pound of nectarines equals:
3-4 fresh medium-size nectarines
2½ cups sliced nectarines
1 pint canned
2 cups diced
A medium sized nectarine has about 90 calories, vitamins A & C and additional nutrients in minor amounts.

NECTARINE SOLE CALIFORNIA

1	lb	fillets of sole, fresh or frozen and thawed
¼	c	butter or margarine
2		fresh nectarines
2-4	T	lemon juice
2	T	minced parsley, optional

Fry sole in half the butter, 2 or 3 minutes each side. Remove to platter; keep warm. Add remaining butter to pan. Add thinly sliced nectarines and lemon juice; heat through. Spoon over fish. Sprinkle with parsley, if desired, garnish with lemon wedges.

Makes 2 or 3 servings.

California Tree Fruit Agreement

NECTARINE ICE

8		to 10 fresh nectarines
1	c	granulated sugar
¼	tsp	salt
½	c	orange juice
2		to 4 T lemon juice
2		egg whites

Peel and slice nectarines to make 4 cups; mash with ¾ **cup** of sugar. Stir in salt and fruit juices. Turn into metal ice cube tray, cover with waxed paper or foil; freeze until nearly firm. Beat egg whites until foamy; gradually add ¼ cup sugar and beat to soft peaks. Gradually beat in nearly frozen fruit mixture. Turn into 2 metal ice cube trays; freeze firm.

Yield: about 1 ½ quarts.

California Tree Fruit Agreement

NECTARINE POTATO PANCAKES

1½	c	grated raw potato
1		fresh nectarine, diced
3		eggs
2	T	flour
¾	tsp	onion salt
		Vegetable oil

Combine potato, nectarine, eggs, flour and onion salt in bowl. Spoon into lightly oiled hot skillet, about ¼ cup mixture for each pancake. Flatten slightly with spatula. Cook over medium-high heat until golden brown, about 1 ½ to 2 minutes on each side. Add a light coating of oil to skillet as needed. Repeat until all batter is used, keeping cooked pancakes warm.

Yield: 9 pancakes.

California Tree Fruit Agreement

181

NECTARINE GLAZED PIE

2/3	c	sugar
3	T	cornstarch
		Dash salt
3		ripe nectarines, peeled, pitted & MASHED
⅓	c	water
1		9-inch baked pastry shell, cooled
6		nectarines,* pitted and DICED
2		nectarines,* pitted and SLICED
		Whipped cream

In a small saucepan combine sugar, cornstarch and salt. Stir in the **mashed** fruit and water. Cook and stir till mixture is thickened and bubbly. Cook and stir 2 minutes more. Remove from heat; cover surface with clear plastic wrap. Set aside to cool. Spread about ¼ cup of the cooled mixture in the bottom of the baked pastry shell. Reserve ⅓ cup of the cooled mixture; set aside. Combine **diced** fruit with remaining mixture, stirring to coat fruit well. Turn into the pastry shell. Top with **sliced** fruit; spoon the reserved ⅓ cup mixture over pie. Cover and chill several hours. To serve, fill center of pie with whipped cream.

*To prevent the fruit from turning brown, dice and slice into a prepared solution of ascorbic acid color keeper or lemon juice mixed with water, drain well before using.

NECTARINE CHEESECAKE PIE   375⁰ — 30 Minutes

2		or 3 fresh nectarines
1		unbaked 9-inch pie shell
3		eggs
½	c	whipping cream
1¼	c	powdered sugar
2		pkgs (3 oz each) cream cheese, softened
1	tsp	grated lemon rind
1	tsp	lemon juice

Slice enough nectarines to measure 1 2/3 cups; arrange in bottom of pie shell. Beat **2** eggs lightly with cream and **1 cup** powdered sugar, pour over fruit. Beat cheese with lemon rind and juice, 1 egg and ¼ cup sugar, gently spoon over cream mixture already in shell. Bake 375⁰ for 30 minutes. Cool thoroughly. Garnish with nectarine slices and, if you wish, a dollop of softened cream cheese.

Makes 6 to 8 servings.

California Tree Fruit Agreement

NECTARINE BREAKFAST FRITTERS

½   c   **buttermilk pancake mix**
⅓   c   **whole milk**
1   **egg**
3   **nectarines, cut into sixths**
        Vegetable oil
        Powdered sugar

Beat pancake mix with milk and egg to get a smooth batter. Add nectarines, stirring to coat. Place enough oil in saucepan to get the depth of 1½ inches and heat to 425° using deep-fat thermometer. Spike nectarine wedges with fork. Allow excess batter to drip off fruit and drop, a few at a time, into hot oil. Cook until lightly browned, about 20 to 30 seconds. Remove from oil with slotted spoon. Drain on paper towels. Sprinkle with powdered sugar to serve.

Makes 4 servings.

California Tree Fruit Agreement

NECTARINE HIGH FIBER BARS

375° — 10 Minutes
+ 20 Minutes

1   c   **butter or margarine, softened**
1   c   **brown sugar, packed**
1⅓ c   **all-purpose flour**
1⅓ c   **whole wheat flour**
1⅓ c   **rolled oats**
1   tsp **cinnamon**
½   tsp **salt**
1¼ c   **fresh nectarines, pitted and chopped finely**

Cream butter with sugar. Mix in flours, oats, cinnamon and salt to get an even moist crumb. Press 3½ cups crumb mixture into bottom of 13x9-inch baking pan. Bake at 375° for 10 minutes. Top with even layer of nectarines. Sprinkle with remaining crumb mixture. Press into nectarine layer. Return to 375° oven and bake for 20 minutes more or until lightly browned. Cool. Cut into bars.

Yield: about 2 dozen bars.

California Tree Fruit Agreement

NECTARINE CRUMB PIE   375⁰ — 55 Minutes

1	c	unsifted flour
½	c	brown sugar, firmly packed
½	c	margarine
½	c	walnuts, chopped
3	T	cornstarch
½	tsp	ground ginger
½	c	light corn syrup
4½		peeled, sliced nectarines
1		unbaked 9-inch pastry shell

In bowl stir together flour and sugar. With pastry blender or 2 knives cut in margarine until crumbs form. Stir in nuts; set aside. In medium bowl mix cornstarch and ginger. Stir in corn syrup until smooth. Add nectarines. Toss to coat. Spoon into pastry shell. Sprinkle crumb mixture on top. Bake 375⁰ for 55 minutes or until golden brown.

Makes 8 servings.

NECTARINE CHEESECAKE COOKIES   350⁰ — 12 Minutes

1	pkg	(8 oz) cream cheese, softened
2	T	sugar
1	tsp	grated lemon peel
2	T	lemon juice
1	T	whole milk
½	tsp	vanilla
		Granola Crust*
1	lg	fresh nectarine, sliced into 20 wedges

Combine cream cheese, sugar, lemon peel, lemon juice, milk and vanilla in a mixer bowl. Beat until smooth. Spread over baked Granola Crust. Arrange nectarine wedges in rows on cheese mixture. Bake at 350⁰ for 12 minutes or until cheese is set. Cool and cut into bars.

Yield: 20 bars.

*Granola Crust: Beat ¾ cup softened butter with ⅓ cup sugar, 3 egg yolks and 1½ cups flour until smooth. Mix in ¾ cup granola. Pat gently into bottom of 13x9-inch baking pan. Bake at 350⁰ for 15 minutes.

California Tree Fruit Agreement

NECTARINE CUSTARD ICE CREAM

2		eggs, beaten
1½	c	whole milk
1	c	sugar
1/8	tsp	salt
1½	tsp	vanilla extract
¼	tsp	almond extract
1½	c	whipping cream
1½	c	nectarine puree

Combine eggs, milk, sugar and salt in saucepan. Cook over low heat, stirring constantly, until mixture coats metal spoon lightly. DO NOT BOIL. Remove from heat; stir in vanilla and almond extracts and cream. Cool. Blanch and peel nectarines; halve or slice, then puree to make 1½ cups. Add to custard mixture. Pour into 2-quart ice cream freezer and freeze according to manufacturer's directions.

California Tree Fruit Agreement

NECTARINE SURFERS' SALAD

2½	c	fresh sliced nectarines
3	c	shredded iceberg lettuce
2	can	(7½ oz each) crab meat, drained and flaked
		OR
1	lb	cooked crab meat
3		or 4 hard-cooked eggs, sliced
1½	c	bread croutons
1		avocado, sliced
¼	c	chopped green onion
½	c	dairy sour cream
¼	c	catsup
1	tsp	Worcestershire
1	tsp	prepared horseradish

Set aside a few slices of nectarines for garnish; place remainder in large salad bowl with lettuce, crab, eggs, croutons, avocado and onion. Gently toss salad, garnish with nectarine slices. Chill. Blend sour cream, catsup, Worcestershire and horseradish in small dish, pass with salad.
Makes 6 to 8 servings.

California Tree Fruit Agreement

NECTARINE FROZEN YOGURT CREME

3		fresh nectarines, chopped
1	c	sugar
2		egg whites
1	T	lemon juice
1	c	whipping cream
½	c	plain yogurt

Combine nectarines, sugar, egg whites and lemon juice in large mixer bowl. Beat with high speed until very fluffy and stiff (approximately 7 minutes). Whip cream until stiff peaks form. Fold whipped cream and yogurt into nectarine mixture. Turn into plastic freezer containers. Cover and freeze until firm. Scoop or spoon into stemmed glasses or dessert dishes. Garnish with additional nectarine wedges and mint sprigs.
Yield: about 2 quarts.

California Tree Fruit Agreement

NECTARINE-CHERRY CHICKEN SALAD

½	c	mayonnaise or salad dressing
2	T	vinegar
2	T	honey
1	tsp	lemon juice
½	tsp	curry powder
1/8	tsp	ground ginger
1/8	tsp	salt
3	c	cooked cubed chicken
1½	c	thinly sliced celery
3	med	nectarines, pitted and sliced
1½	c	dark sweet cherries, halved and pitted
1	T	thinly sliced green onion
½	c	toasted, slivered almonds
		Lettuce
		Fresh nectarine wedges, optional

Combine mayonnaise or salad dressing, vinegar, honey, lemon juice, curry powder, ginger and salt; set aside. In a large bowl combine the cooked chicken, celery, nectarines, cherries and green onion. Pour the dressing over chicken mixture; toss lightly to mix. Chill several hours. At serving time, add the toasted almonds and toss with salad. Serve in a lettuce-lined bowl. Trim top of salad with a few nectarine wedges, if desired.
Makes 6 servings.

NECTARINE FRUIT SALAD TOSS-UP

¼	c	sugar
3	T	vinegar
2	T	water
¾	T	celery salt
¾	tsp	paprika
¾	tsp	dry mustard
2/3	c	salad oil
2	c	sliced nectarines
2	c	cut up pineapple
2	c	grapes, seeded
6	c	torn mixed greens

In saucepan combine sugar, vinegar, water, celery salt, paprika and mustard. Heat and stir till sugar dissolves; cool. Transfer mixture to small mixer bowl. Add oil in a slow stream, beating till thick. Cover and chill. To serve, arrange fruits atop greens. Pour dressing over - toss to coat.

Makes 12 servings.

NECTARINE TOMATO HERB JAM

4		fresh nectarines
5	c	sugar
2	med	tomatoes
2	T	tarragon-flavor white wine vinegar
½	tsp	basil, crumbled
2		pouches (3 oz each) liquid pectin

Pit nectarines and cut fruit into large pieces to measure 1 quart. Combine with **1 cup** sugar in large saucepan. Let stand a few minutes until juice begins to form. Bring to boiling over high heat. Boil 10 minutes, stirring frequently. Meanwhile, blanch tomatoes in boiling water 10 seconds to loosen skins. Remove skins and cores and dice fruit in large pieces to measure 1½ cups. Add to nectarine mixture along with remaining **4 cups** sugar, vinegar and basil. Bring to a full rolling boil (a boil that cannot be stirred down). Boil hard 1 minute. Remove from heat and stir in pectin. Pour into clean, hot jars filling with jam to ½ inch from top. Adjust lids and set jars in canner or on rack in deep kettle. Add boiling water to cover jars 1 to 2 inches. Bring back to a boil and process 10 minutes. Remove from canner at once and set on heat-proof surface to cool before storing.

Yield: 6 cups.

California Tree Fruit Agreement

NECTARINE FRYING PAN SALAD

		Fresh spinach leaves
2		**fresh nectarines**
2-3	T	**thinly sliced green onion**
4		**slices bacon**
¼	c	**cider vinegar**
½	tsp	**salt**
1	T	**brown sugar**

Wash and tear spinach leaves from stems; tear large leaves into pieces and pack down in cup to measure 3 to 4 cups. Pat with paper towels to remove excess moisture. Coarsely chop nectarines to yield 1 cup. In a bowl or plastic bag combine the spinach, nectarines and onions. Cut bacon into ½-inch pieces and fry until crisp in large skillet. Drain crisp bits and add to spinach combination. Pour all but 2 tablespoons of bacon drippings from pan. Add vinegar, salt and brown sugar to remaining drippings. Heat just to simmering. Remove from heat and add spinach combination; toss well. Serve at once while slightly warm.

Makes 4 to 6 servings.

California Tree Fruit Agreement

Happiness adds and multiplies as we divide it with others.

A. Nielen

NECTARINE JAM

3	lbs	**fully ripe nectarines**
2	T	**lemon juice**
7½	c	**sugar**
1		**bottle (6 oz) liquid pectin**

Peel and pit fully ripe nectarines. Chop fine or grind and measure 4 cups into a very large saucepan; add lemon juice. Add sugar to nectarines and mix well. Place over high heat, bring to a full rolling boil and boil hard 1 minute, stirring constantly. Remove from heat and at once stir in pectin. Skim off foam. Stir and skim for 5 minutes to cool slightly and prevent floating fruit. Ladle quickly into sterilized jars. Cover at once with 1/8 inch hot paraffin.

Yield: about 10 half-pints.

NECTARINE STRUDEL

400° — 30 Minutes

1	pkg	(10 oz) frozen patty shells, thawed
4	med	fresh nectarines, sliced
¾	c	crushed macaroons
¼	c	dark seedless raisins, optional
½	tsp	grated lemon peel
1		egg yolk, beaten with 1 tsp water
		Granulated sugar
		Sliced natural almonds

Press patty shells together. Roll out on lightly floured surface to 20 x 12- inch rectangle. Transfer to lightly greased shallow baking pan. Mix nectarines, macaroons, raisins and lemon peel. Spoon mixture lengthwise along center of rectangle, leaving about 3 inches of dough uncovered on both sides. Fold dough over filling to enclose it completely. Pinch ends closed. Curve strip into a horseshoe shape. Brush with egg yolk mixture. Sprinkle with sugar and almonds. Bake at 400° for 30 minutes or until golden brown.

California Tree Fruit Agreement

NECTARINE BREAD

350° — 55 Minutes

½	c	shortening
2/3	c	sugar
2	lg	eggs
1	c	fresh peeled, finely chopped nectarines
2	c	sifted all-purpose flour
2½	tsp	baking powder
¾	tsp	salt
1/8	tsp	ground cardamon

Cream shortening and sugar together well. Add eggs and nectarines and beat well (batter may appear curdled). Resift flour with baking powder, salt and cardamon. Add to nectarine mixture and stir just until all of flour is moistened. Turn into greased loaf pan (8½ x 4 x 3-inch). Bake below center at 350° for 55 - 60 minutes or until loaf tests done. Let stand 10 minutes, then turn out onto wire rack to cool. Cool thoroughly before cutting.
    Yield: 1 loaf.

California Tree Fruit Agreement

NECTARINE-PEAR JAM

2	c	ripe finely chopped nectarines
2	c	ripe, finely chopped, peeled pears
4	tsp	finely shredded orange peel
¼	c	orange juice
3	T	lemon juice
7½	c	sugar
1	pkg	(2 pouches) liquid fruit pectin

In an 8 or 10-quart saucepot, combine nectarines, pears, orange peel, orange juice and lemon juice. Stir in sugar. Bring mixture to a full rolling boil; boil hard, uncovered, for 1 minute, stirring constantly. Remove from heat; stir in the pectin. Quickly skim off foam with a metal spoon. Ladle jam at once into hot, clean half-pint jars, leaving ¼-inch headspace. Wipe jar rims; adjust lids and process in water bath for 15 minutes.

Yield: 10 half pints.

NECTARINE NO-COOK JAM

2¼	lbs	fully ripe nectarines
1	tsp	ascorbic acid crystals
5½	c	sugar
1	c	light corn syrup
2		pouches (3 oz ea) liquid fruit pectin
⅓	c	lemon juice

Peel, pit and thinly slice nectarines. Add ascorbic acid crystals. Crush, one layer at a time, to let juice flow freely. Measure 2¾ cups. In large bowl stir together nectarines, sugar and corn syrup until well blended. Let stand 10 minutes. In small bowl mix pectin and lemon juice. Stir into nectarine mixture. Stir vigorously 3 minutes. Ladle into freezer containers leaving ½-inch headspace (no paraffin needed). Cover with tight lids. Let stand at room temperature until set. Freeze; transfer to refrigerator as needed.

Yield: 8 half-pints.

To own a bit of ground, to scratch it with a hoe, to plant seeds and watch the renewal of life - this is the commonest delight of the race, the most satisfactory thing a man can do.

Charles Dudley Warner

NECTARINE-PEACH JAM

1½	lbs	ripe nectarines
1½	lbs	ripe peaches
1	pkg	(1¾ oz) powdered fruit pectin
2	T	lemon juice
3½	c	sugar
1	c	light corn syrup

Peel, pit and quarter peaches and nectarines. Finely chop and measure 1½ cups of each. In 8-quart stainless steel or enamel saucepot stir together nectarines, peaches, pectin and lemon juice until well blended. Stirring constantly, bring to full rolling boil. Stir in sugar and corn syrup. Return to full rolling boil and stirring constantly, boil rapidly 1 minute. Remove from heat; skim surface. Immediately ladle into clean hot jars leaving ¼ inch headspace. Adjust lids and process in boiling water bath 5 minutes.

Yield: 6 half-pints.

Index By Category

Pastries

Salads and Congeals

Desserts

Preserves

Ice Cream and Beverages

Miscellaneous

Calorie-Conscious

Microwave

Nectarines

California Tree Fruit Agreement

Georgia Peach Commission

National Peach Council

South Carolina Department of Agriculture

South Carolina Peach Council

My Prayer

Help me to walk with Thee through every day,
Be thou my guide and leader of my way;
Lest in my weakness I should from thee stray,
Send me Thy grace.

May I be swift some broken dream to mend,
Of one who is a stranger or a friend,
And may I when the day has reached its end
Still see Thy face.

Help me, in my fellowmen, the good to see
And may I through this day be led by Thee
To see the doors of opportunity
That always open lie.

Make me an instrument to do Thy will;
Take Thou my life and with Thy wonder fill
My very being, Father, may I still
Always on Thee rely.

David Ogletree